for my sister

# Extreme Graphics

Edited By
Kathleen Ziegler and Nick Greco

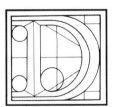

## Dimensional Illustrators, Inc.

**HBI**
**Hearst Books International**

**ExtremeGraphics**

**First Published 1998 by**
**DIMENSIONAL ILLUSTRATORS, INC.**
**FOR HEARST BOOKS INTERNATIONAL**
1350 Avenue of the Americas
New York, NY 10019

ISBN: 1-885660-15-4

**Distributed in the U.S. and Canada by**
**WATSON-GUPTILL PUBLICATIONS**
1515 Broadway
New York, NY 1003
800-451-1741 Phone
732-363-4511 in NJ,AK,HI
732-363-0338 Fax

ISBN: 0-8230-6617-7

**Distributed throughout the rest of the world by**
**HEARST BOOKS INTERNATIONAL**
1350 Avenue of the Americas
New York, NY 10019 USA
212-261-6795 Fax

**First Published in Germany by**
**NIPPAN**
Nippon Shuppan Hanbai
Deutschland GmbH
Krefelder Str. 85
D-40549 Dusseldorf
0211-5048089 Telephone
0211-5049326 Fax

ISBN: 3-931884-33-3

(c) Copyright 1998 by Dimensional Illustrators, Inc. and
Hearst Books International

**Address Direct Mail Sales to**
DIMENSIONAL ILLUSTRATORS, INC.
362 Second Street Pike / Suite 112
Southampton, PA 18966 USA
Email: dimension@3dimillus.com
Wedsite: http://www.3dimillus.com
215-953-1415 Phone
215-953-1697 Fax

*Printed in Singapore*

## ExtremeGraphics Credits

### Creative Designer/Creative Editor
Kathleen Ziegler
Dimensional Illustrators, Inc.

### Executive Editor
Nick Greco
Dimensional Illustrators, Inc.

### Book, Jacket Cover Design & Typography
Deborah Davis

### Copywriters
Nick Greco
Cathy Fishel/Catharine & Sons

### Copy Consultants
Cathy Fishel/Catharine & Sons
Leona Mangol

### Cover Image
Michael Morgenstern

# Table of Contenets

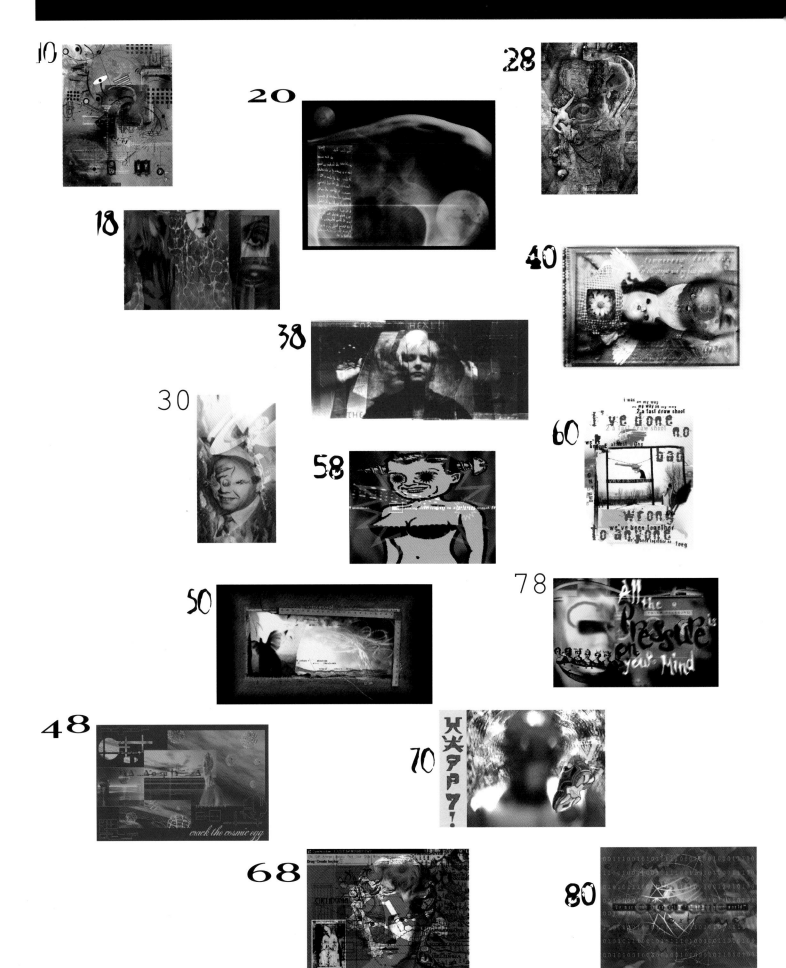

10

28

20

18

40

38

30

60

58

50

78

48

70

68

80

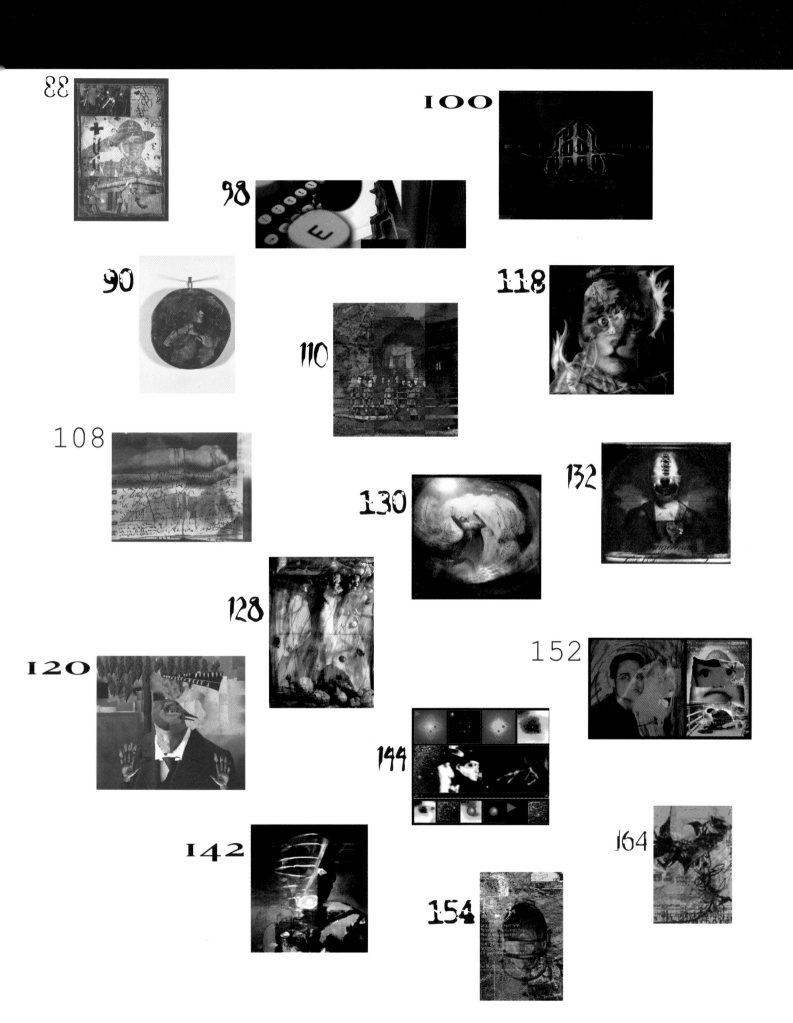

88

100

98

90

118

110

108

132

130

128

152

120

144

142

164

154

# ExtremeGraphics

ExtremeGraphics features the work of more than 30 exceptional visionaries who **push the limits** of their imagery **beyond the genre** of digital illustration. The

images contained in this premiere edition represent the newest wave of digital creatives. Their provocative work challenges the viewer to experience the **inner passion** of the artist and decipher the **surrealistic imagery** of an elite electronic design community.

This invitation-only publication includes the work of artists from the United States, Brazil, Canada, England, Finland, Italy and Japan. Their **creative license** has brought to fruition the versatility and infinite capabilities of computer-generated artistry. Never before have artists enjoyed such **freedom of artistic** expression.

Each of their images takes the viewer into a **cosmos**

**of metaphors and symbolism** through

haunting fragments of compositional elements. From fluid

and impressionistic to **bizarre and**

**enigmatic**, the artwork strikes the viewer at different

levels of intensity.

9

The layered, interwoven images featured in this book

reflect the **powerful capabil-**

**ities** of the computer's unlimited potential.

The computer-as-tool allows their actual production;

however, the medium is far more than

"**JUST A TOOL**." The computer's speed and

flexibility also seem to serve

**as a catharsis** that opens the creative

floodgates and allows the artists' ideas to flow into

imagery without getting muddied by physical restraints.

The **results are absolutely** unprecedented.

Kathleen Ziegler and Nick Greco
Dimensional Illustrators, Inc.

# Speed Setting

self Promotion purpose

digital area digital creative

Jeff Brice

software

Adobe Photoshop, FreeHand

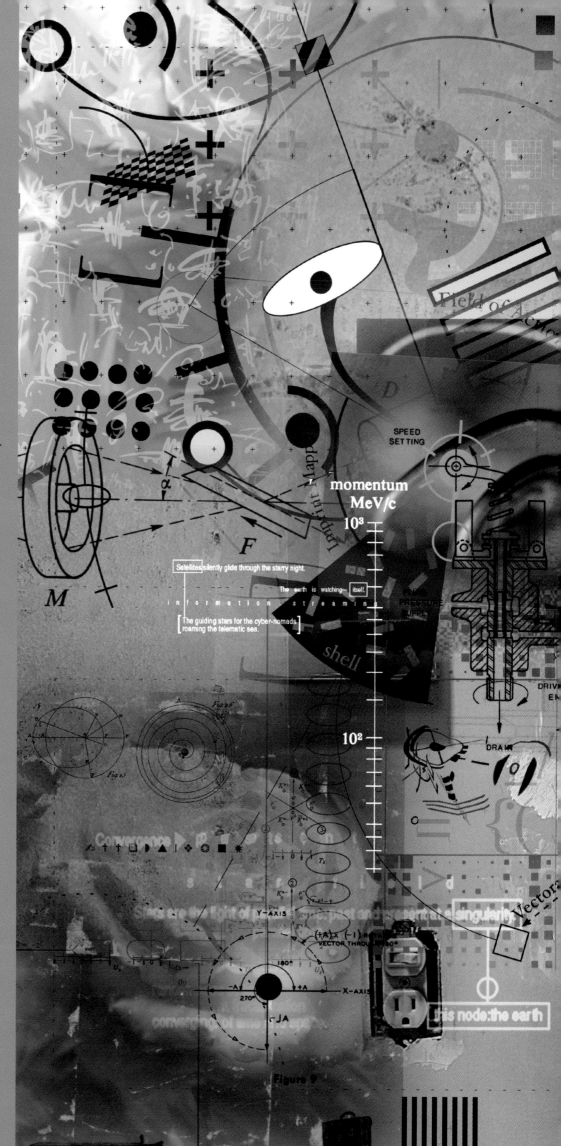

Jeff Brice's provocative supposition that digital art sits in that uneasy place between modernist and post-modernist, image, object and the real and the simulated is evident in Speed Setting, a visual poem.

According to the artist, the work captures a heartbeat in time, but it is a moment built on the solid foundation of history. Just as the binary code that executed the image still exists, time has passed yet remains. Brice's ability to blend fine art, commercial art and writing is at the center of his creative genius.

A painter turned digital illustrator, Brice created this piece of visual rhetoric in FreeHand and imported it into Adobe Photoshop. He feels that the art reveals the linear and circular velocity of the time it takes any action to occur.

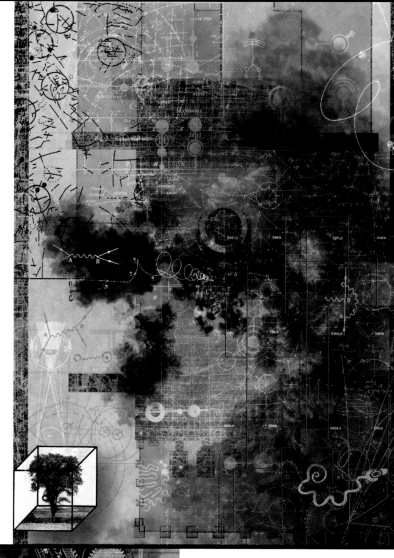

self Promotion

purpose

digital creative

Nature

Jeff Brice

Adobe
Photoshop,
FreeHand

software

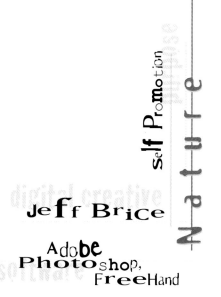

digital creative

Jeff Brice

software

Adobe
Photoshop,
FreeHand

self Promotion

purpose

Gate

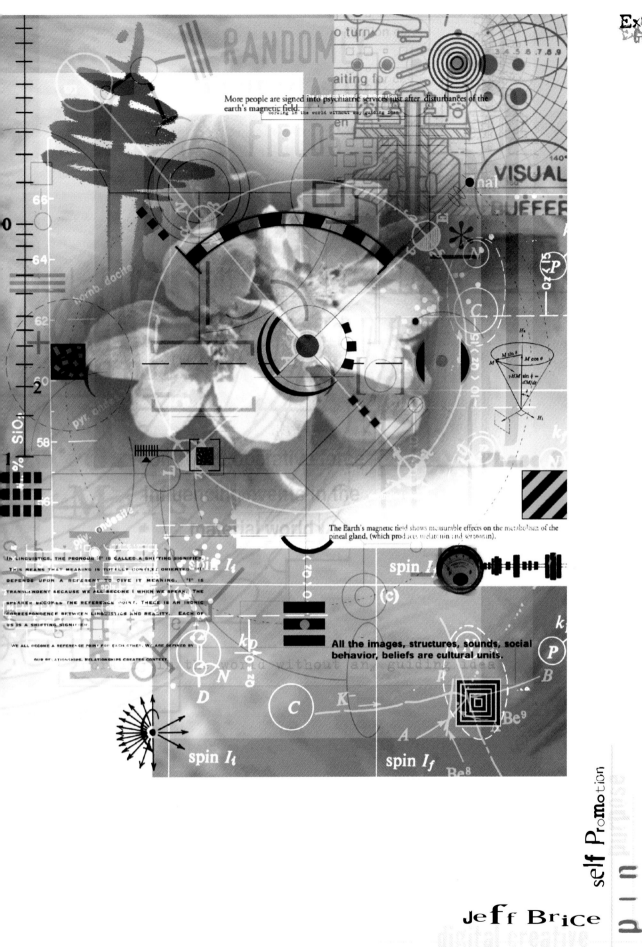

self Promotion
*purpose*

Primum Mobile

Adobe Photoshop
*software*

Alessandro
Bavari
*digital creative*

14

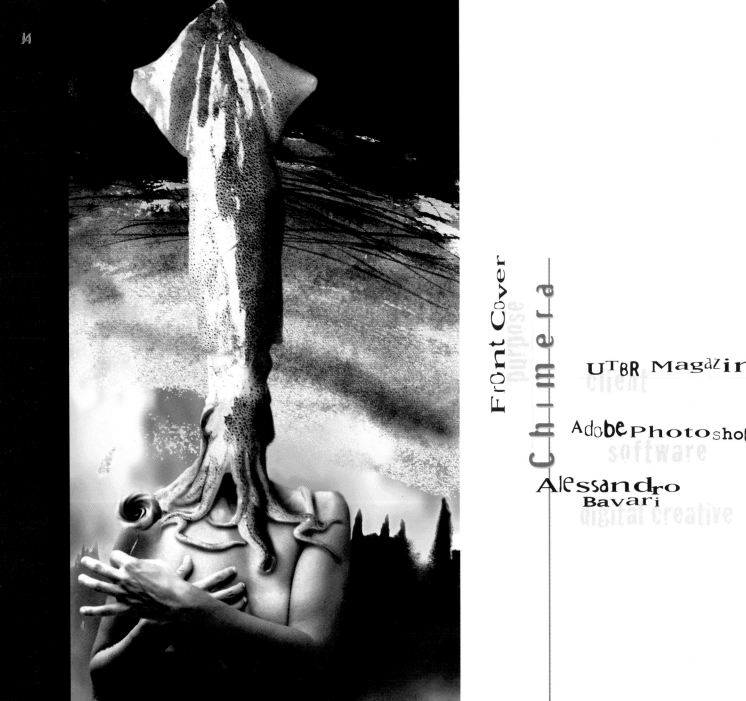

Front Cover
*purpose*

Chimera

UTBR Magazine
*client*

Adobe Photoshop
*software*

Alessandro
Bavari
*digital creative*

self Promotion
inhouse

Le Sirene

digital
creative

Alessandro
Bavari

software

AdobePhotoshop

Portfolio Piece
inhouse

Angel Interpretations #7

scott w. Petty
digital creative

self Promotion
client

AdobePhotoshop
Illustrator software

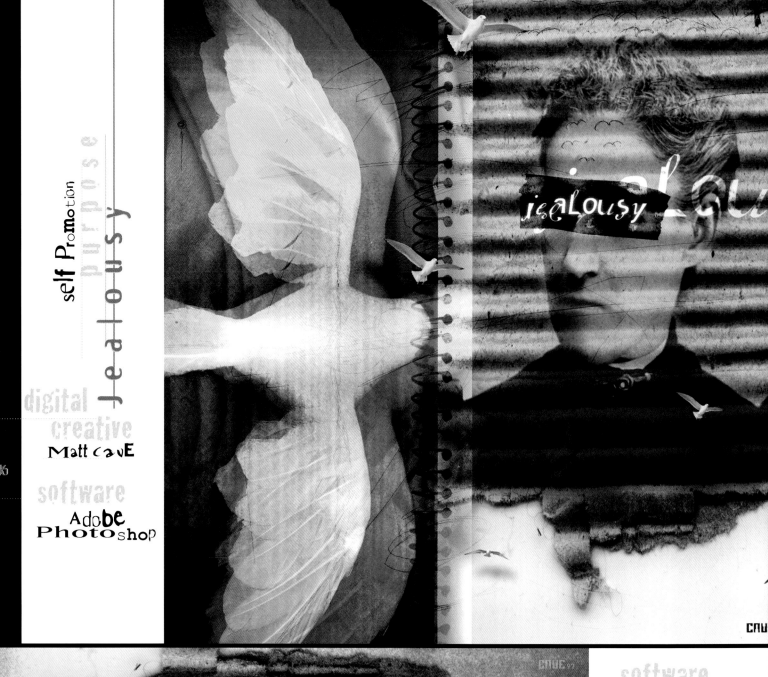

self **P**romotion

purpose

jealousy

digital
creative

Matt CavE

software

Ado**be**
Photoshop

THIS IS ART

software

Ado**be**
Photoshop

digital
creative

Matt CavE

self **P**romotion

purpose

This Is Art

Matt cavE

digital creative

d8 Magazine

client

Adobe
Photoshop

software

Editorial purpose

HTML

The components of Pascos' work are diverse. He incorporates Pola paintings, and will even scan 3-D objects to extract their texture. manipulated, painted, distorted and enhanced in Adobe Photos inviting the spectator to indulge. The more

Greg Pascos prefers to build his images with seemingly unrelated elements to form a sense sub of Greg Pascos prefers to build his images with seemingly unrelated elements to form a sense sub cons Greg Pascos prefers to build his images with seemingly unrelated elements to form a sense invitation to th was created as an invitation to th invitation

35mm and digital photos. He scans his personal drawings and
ything is **dramatically**
The FINISHED COLLAGE is brimming with imagery,
ewer studies the work, the more information is **derived.**

Promotional FoldeR & InVitation
**purpose**

# 1 face

Greg Pascos
digital creative

Adobe Photoshop
**software**

Concept's Salon, Esthétique
**client**

conscious image
rather than literal meaning. This **fluid, impressionistic** image was **created** as an
pening of a health and beauty **spa.**

Artwork from Millennium series

continuum

digital creative
digital creative
digital creative

software
Adobe Photoshop, Fractal Poser

Lisa A. Johnston

purpose
self Promotion
client

The human **form**, suspended by a powerful force in **SPACE**, creates the image of "**conti**...

the title of this montage, conceived by Lisa A. Johnston. Six photos, collaged in Adobe Pho...

together to **communicate the immensit**...

**discovery**. The composite is part of a series titled, **"millennium**...

"a virtual pageant of digital montage probing man's **direction** into ou...

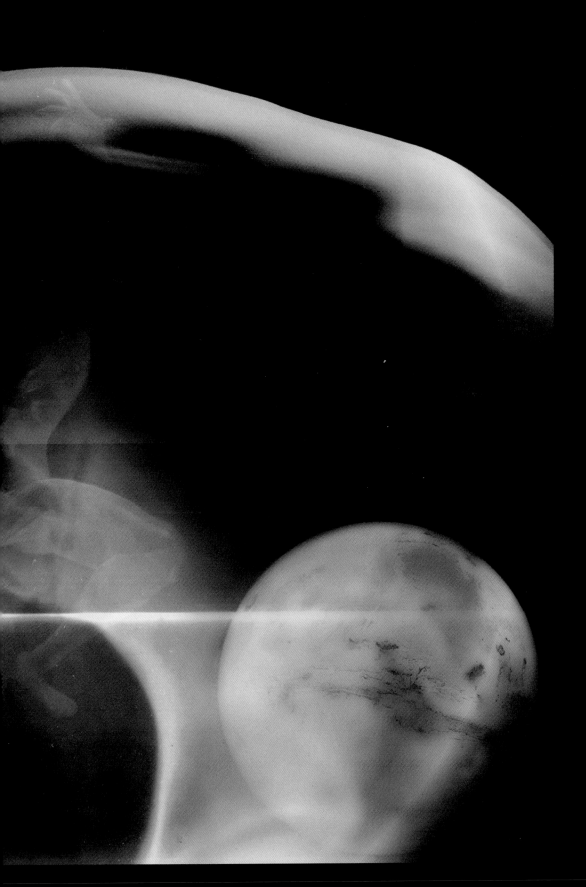

Her theme is exploration and discovery: The distorted handwriting may be a scientist's hurried scribble, or it might be careful notes on the state of the

## Universe

"um," and Kai's Power Tools, work of calls "a virtual page ch Johnston calls ture."

Man's **struggle** for enlightenment is **sym**bolized *an* **X**ray *by* of a pelvis coupled with the *strain of the Atlas-like figure.*

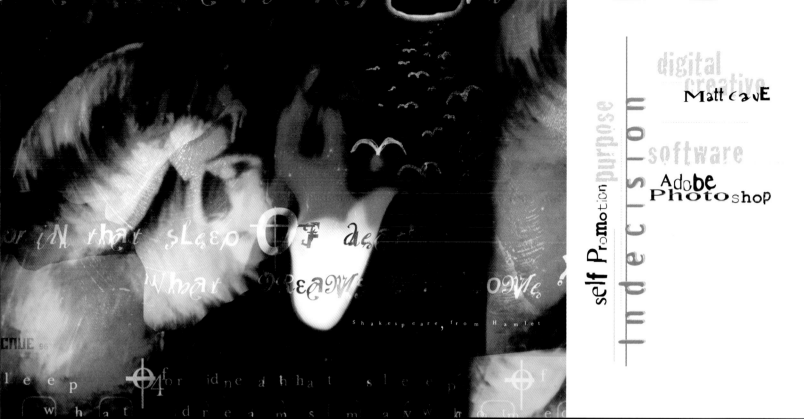

digital creative

Matt cavE

self ProMotion

V - 3 purpose

Adobe software
Photoshop

self Promotion

Matt Cave

Adobe Photoshop

digital creative

software

23

Portfolio Piece

purpose

Byron

digital creative

Scott W. Petty

client

self Promotion

Adobe Photoshop, Illustrator

software

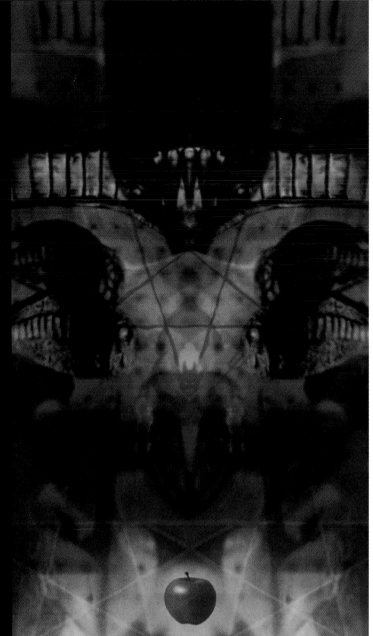

obser**V**ation of **N**ike **Cu**lt**U**re purpose

# **A B**r**a**n**d** N**e**w **Ga**r**d**e**n**

digital creative

Pau**L** Wa**t**son

software

Ado**be**Photo**shop**

self **P**r**o**m**o**tion purpose

**R a**

digital creative

**J**ohn **J**. **Hi**ll

software

Ado**be**Photo**shop**

X**V**

poster **purpose** Ascension

JohnJ.Hill
digital creative

TopCow Productions
client

software
AdobePhotoshop

Concert poster **purpose** Ween

PauL watson
digital creative

client
WeeN

software
AdobePhotoshop

ween
WITH DOO RAG
OCTOBER 23
PHOENIX CONCERT THEATRE
CAUTION: FILLINGS HOT

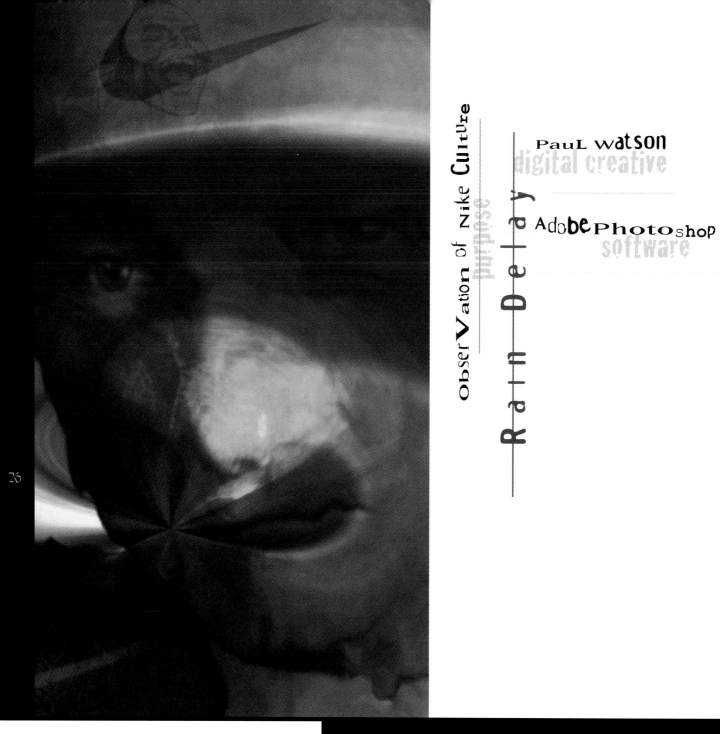

obserVation of Nike Culture
purpose

Rain Delay

PauL watSon
digital creative

AdobePhotoshop
software

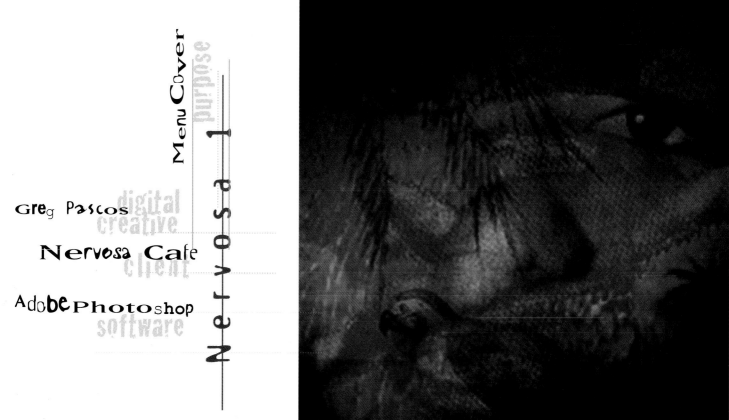

MenuCover
purpose

Nervosa 1

Greg Pascos
digital creative

Nervosa Cafe
client

AdobePhotoshop
software

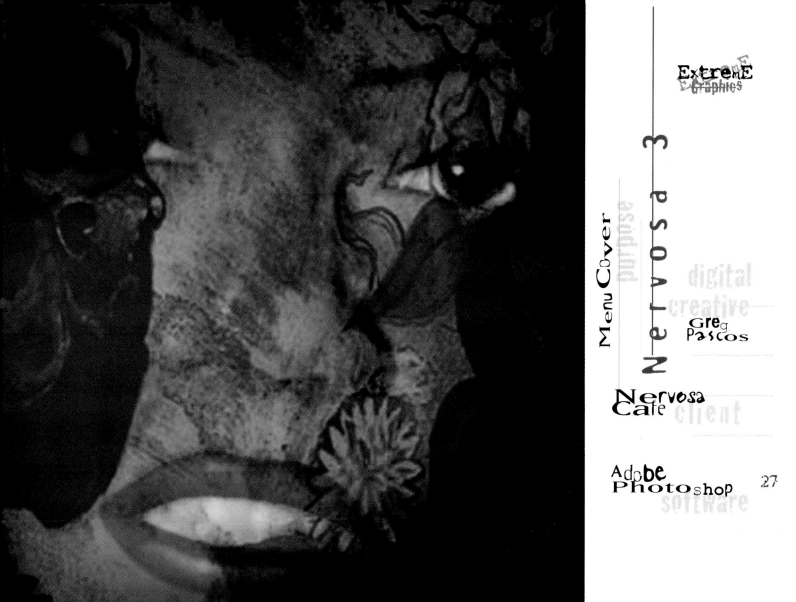

ExtremE
Graphics

Nervosa 3

Menu Cover
purpose

digital
creative
Greg
Pascos

Nervosa
Cafe client

Adobe
Photoshop
software

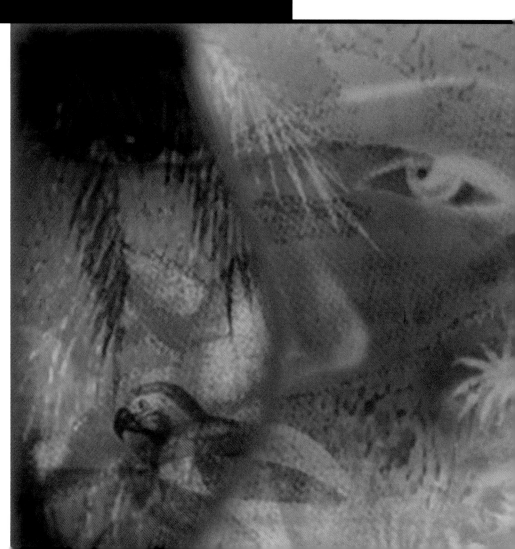

Menu Cover
purpose

Nervosa 2

Greg Pascos
digital
creative

Nervosa Cafe

client

software

Adobe Photoshop

This **kneaded mass** of imagery was created by Domenic Ali to explore the soft**ware's** ability to integrate seamlessly independent images.

For this and other works, the artist will spend **days** (or even weeks) collecting **objects** and pictures with no particular theme guiding each selection. His goal is to create art that ~~strikes~~ the viewer as "photographically coherent" yet its meaning remains **enigmatic and open.** His work is complex, artistically influenced by Dada and surrealism, as well as **chaos theory** and **psychoanalytic** thought.

The image, titled **"The Feeding,"** was formed in Adobe Photoshop using scanned photos; **the background was generated in Terrazzo.**

As the photographs are melded, Ali develops a narrative with the viewer. The **gruesome mass** could be an enormous, **carnivorous creature** stalking its prey or a **lethal microbe** caught in the act of infection.

The scale simply is not clear.

Fine Art purpose

The digital collage

Domenic Ali digital creative

Adobe Photoshop software

Immense switches in the normal scale of the elements abstracts the scene so much it becomes visible from any angle. Watson used Adobe Photoshop to assemble his images and, experimenting with layering, he achieved a bizarre result. Subtle transparency, overexposure, and a warm palette are accented with cool highlights. The fragments are superimpose over graphic and ORGanic elements. Watson notes that the print reflects his view that music is an essential part of the creative process.

This freeze-frame of chaos, an image created for a concert poster by Paul Watson for the band "Guided by Voices" brings together everyday objects in nonsensical ways so they assume new meanings. According to the artist, space travelers encounter a less, abstract dimension. Lured by voices, the ship is entangled in planets and evolving frogs in a fiery outer space. An anonymous head and collars become the spaceship, and the eyes mirror a frog and tadpoles.

Concert poster

purpose

Guided by Voices

digital creative

software

Paul Watson

Adobe Photoshop

client

Guided by Voices

Alessandro Bavari

self Promotion

purpose

Harpyial

digital
creative

Adobe Photoshop

software

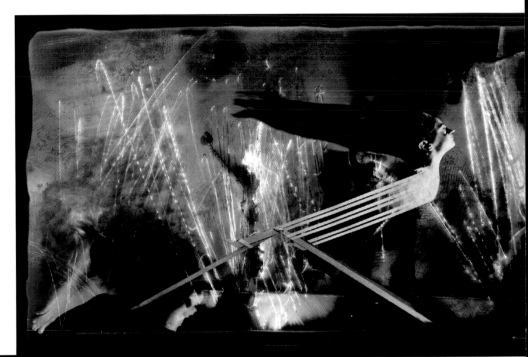

digital
creative

Domenic Ali

Adobe Photoshop

software

Fine Art purpose

Remembrance

ExtremE

Domenic Ali

digital creative

AdobePhotoshop

software

Fine Art

Modern life

digital
creative

Domenic Ali

software

Adobe
Photoshop

Fine Art

purpose

The Arrival

Video Presentation

MercurioAdolescente

digital
creative

Alessandro Bavari

client
software

Direct 2
Brain

Adobe
Photoshop

Fine Art purpose

The Confessional

digital
creative

Domenic Ali

Adobe
Photoshop

software

self Promotion

digital creative

Alessandro
Bavari

software

Ado**be**
Photoshop

Reliquario

UT**BR** Magazine

client

Ado**be**Photoshop

software

Alessandro
Bavari

digital

creative

FrOnt COver

defense

Oread

self Promotion

purpose

Window Vision

digital creative

Lisa A. Johnston

software

Adobe Photoshop

Editorial-Book Cover Documentary

purpose

Life

Kip Henrie

digital creative

client

self Promotion

software

Adobe Photoshop
Illustrator

37

self Promotion

purpose

Haidou

Alessandro
Bavari

digital creative
software

AdobePhotoshop

He uses Adobe Photoshop, darkroom **mani pulation** of his

than by photography, Ferguson likes to include **textural elements** in his work, eve

believable, **multi-layere**d portrait of personal em **power** n

The success of **healing power** through alternativ

Health," by Scott Ferguson. The subject removes h

**strength** of her inner will to fue

...tos and traditional collage to create his work. Inspired more by illustration and **painting**

...porating **scratches and tears.** The result here is a

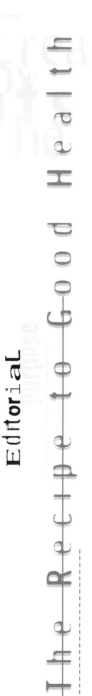

...edicine is portrayed in "The Recipe to Good

...from the **GHOSTED** shadow of her illness, using the

**transformation.**

ment.

self **P**romotion **purpose**

# Memory

digital creative **software**

Ado**be** Photoshop **I**llustrator

**client** K**ip** H**en**r**ie**

s**e**lf **P**romotion

## disin-tegrat

Henrie, who is inspired by old photography and C i n **EM A** , tries to **disintegrate** technology and make high tech look **antiquated**. Here, the girl's **memories** begin with the t o y a n d i t s security. The R**EM**E**M B**R**A**N**CE** within the **doll con**tinues to **f l o w** to her as t**i**me passes

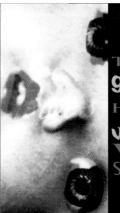

The **unblinking,** gone by that alw Henrie. Created **vibrancy and su** **WORDS** fro SCIOUS as she sl

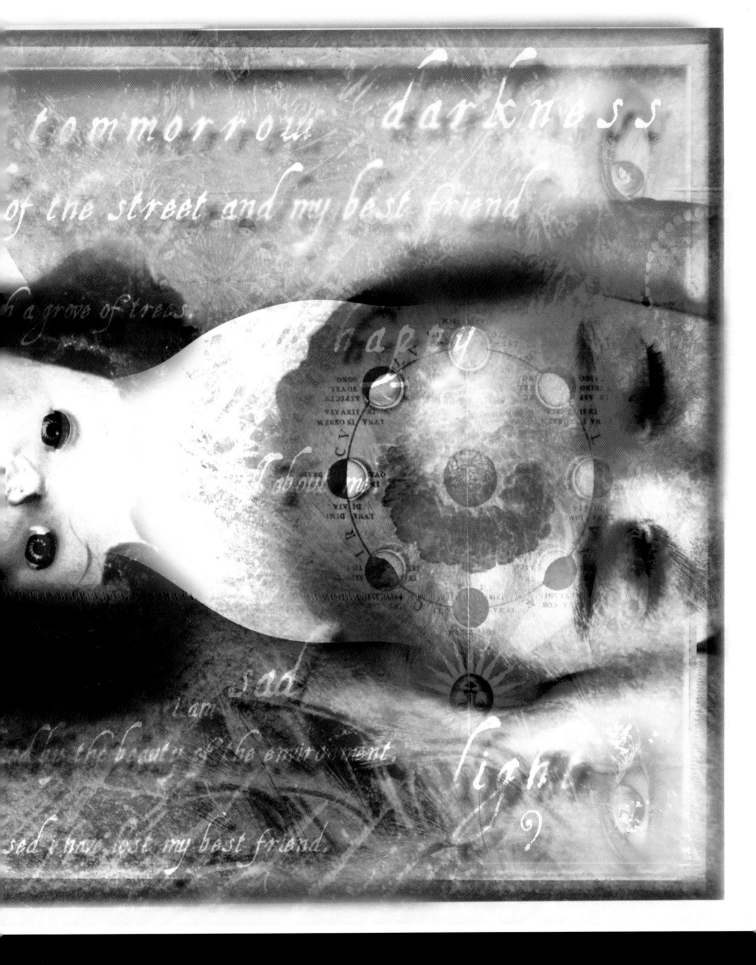

tommorrow darkness

of the street and my best friend

a grove of trees.

happy

sad

i am

the beauty of the environment

light

?

sed i have lost my best friend.

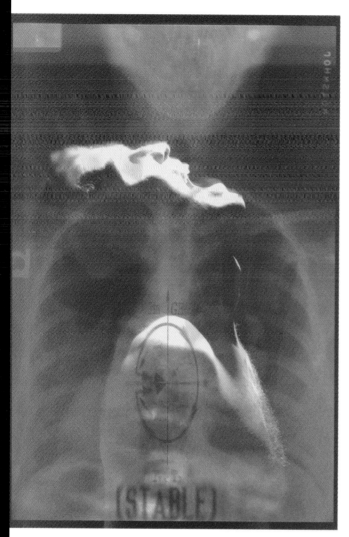

(STABLE)

self Promotion
purpose
Transform Method

Lisa A. Johnston

digital creative

software

Adobe
Photoshop

self Promotion
Mind purpose

digital creative

Lisa A. Johnston

Adobe
Photoshop,
FreeHand
software

DISCRETE TIME SYSTEMS TRANSFORM METHOD

self Promotion

purpose

Stable

digital creative

Lisa A. Johnston

Adobe software
Photoshop
Kai's power Tools

43

self Promotion

purpose

Hands of Dust

digital creative

Lisa A. Johnston

software

Adobe
Photoshop

Scott Ferguson

digital creative
client

Discover Magazine: Vital Signs

Adobe Photoshop, Painter

software

Editorial

Dystonia purpose

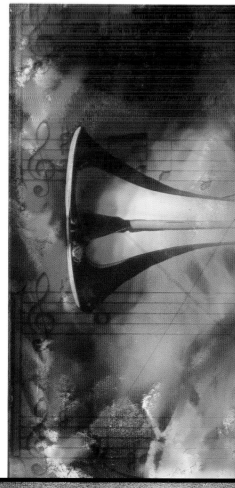

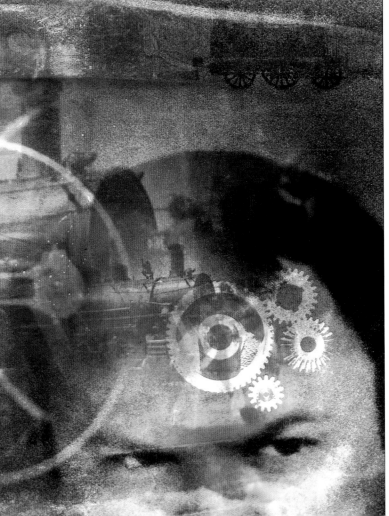

**Editorial**

Train

digital creative

client

software

ScOtt FerguSon

DisCover Magazine: VitaL SigNS

AdobePhotoshop

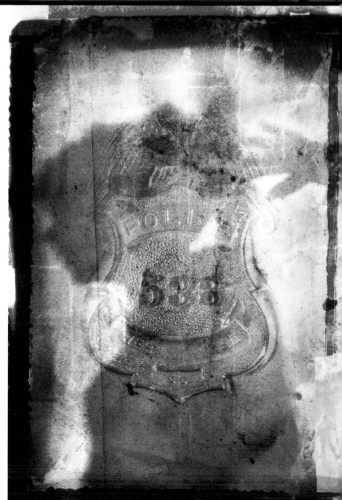

To Protect and To Serve

Editorial *purpose*

Scott Ferguson

digital creative

client

DisCover Magazine: Vital Signs

software

AdobePhotoshop

**Editorial**

Porphyria

Scott Ferguson

digital creative

Discover Magazine: Vital Signs

client

Adobe Photoshop

software

Lobby Display

Crack The Cosmic Egg

Tony Schanuel Digital Creative

client
K&S Photographics

software
Live Picture, Bryce, Adobe Photoshop

The graphic impact of Tony Schanuel's cosmic imagery goes beyond its unusual imagery. Commissioned for a local professional photo lab and imaging center, the piece reproduced as a display graphic for

Assigned to showcase the center'

The influences of **several** inspir

UsingLive Picture and Adobe Photosh

frontier is not **outer** **space**, b

experiencing our relationsh

The graphic
Schanuel's "Crack
the Cosmic Egg"
montage goes
beyond its unusual
imagery.
Commissioned for
a local professional
photo lab and
imaging center, the
piece
was ultimately
reproduced as a
30 x 40-inch
display graphic for
the center's lobby
area.

ity to work with digital files, Schanuel was encouraged to soar creatively to new cosmic heights. onal figures in his life–Dali and Magruitte–are evident. o create the image, the artist awakens his belief that the last ner space. Schanuel insists that we must discover new ways of ith all things.

$33 = f \bullet x \neg \emptyset \yen \emptyset \pi / 12 \degree \mathring{a} \cdots$

$f \Delta \hat{}\ o\ddot{}\degree \neg \Delta \neg ... æ \neg ... æ ...$

*crack the cosmic egg*

CRITICAL amount of
and video work -
ve creativity by pro-
personal study titled
Minefield.

Personal study
purpose

Minefield

digital

John Hill
digital creative

software

Adobe Photoshop

50

Meter

5 T dum p tru

After an **intense** amount of web design and video work, John J. Hill relieved his pent-up illustrative crea

personal study, titled **"Minefield."** He began with one of the **smallest elen**

the assembly-a bird photographed for an earlier project-and slowly a

The **final Puzzle** was pieced together in

Adobe Photoshop. The last object added was laying on the desk in front of him-a well-**worn ruler**.

After an intense amount of web design and video wc
Hill relieved his pent-up illustrative creativity by produ-
Minefield He began
as pieced together i

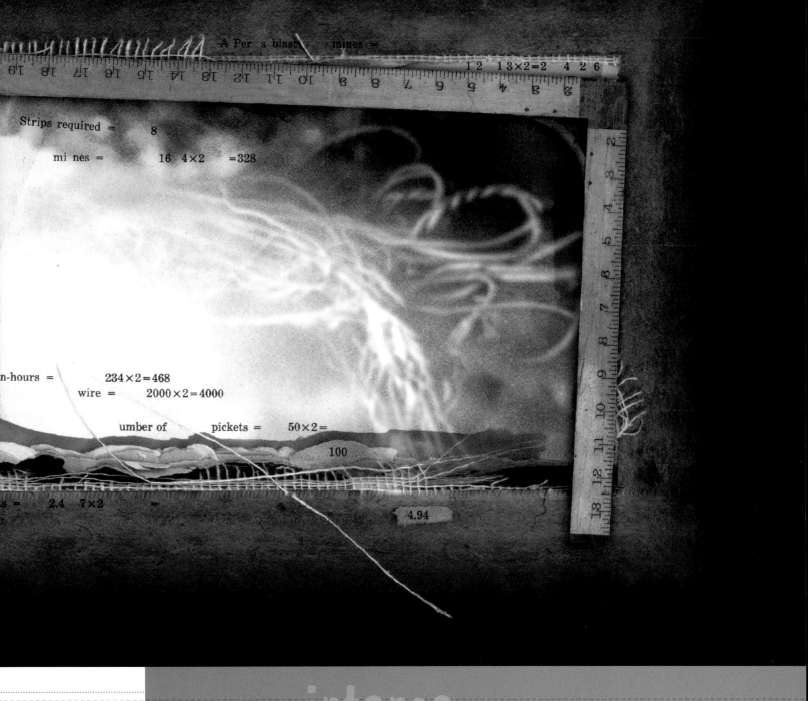

Hill believes that the digital aspect of his work should be invisible and that ~~composition~~, not content, is the key to a successful image. For this print, unrelated found objects and photos are layered, then multiplied, one on top of the last, thereby creating areas of ~~rich,~~ dense color. The result is an electronic image that does not look digital; instead, it feels real, as if one could reach through the window ...and touch the bird in flight.

producing this

John J.

nts in

re scanned objects.

Editorial **purpose**

# Wired Future

digital creative
**Jeff Brice**

Wired Magazine
client

**Adobe** Photoshop,
FReeHand
software

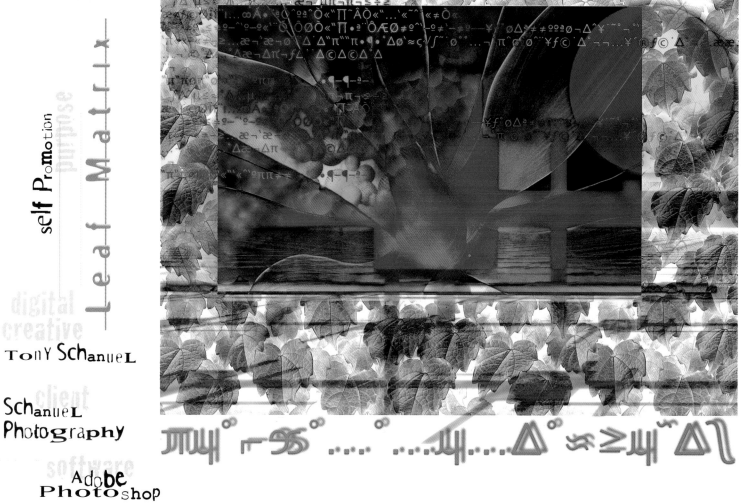

self Promotion **purpose**

# Leaf Matrix

digital creative

**Tony Schanuel**

Schanuel
Photography
client

software
**Adobe** Photoshop

self Promotion

ufo

Jeff Brice

Adobe Photoshop,
FreeHand

53

CD Covers

focus 27

Tony Schanuel

The Monroe
Institute

Adobe
Photoshop,
Live Picture,
Bryce

2001Ω=focus 27 fß

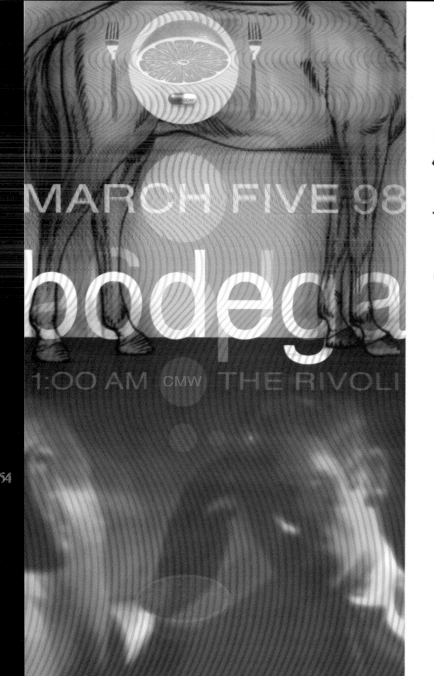

MARCH FIVE 98

bodega

1:00 AM CMW THE RIVOLI

54

Concert poster

Bodega

digital creative
cheap
software

Paul watson

vibra Cobra Records

Adobe Photoshop

Bullfighter

self Promotion
purpose

digital creative
software

Greg Pascos

Adobe Photoshop

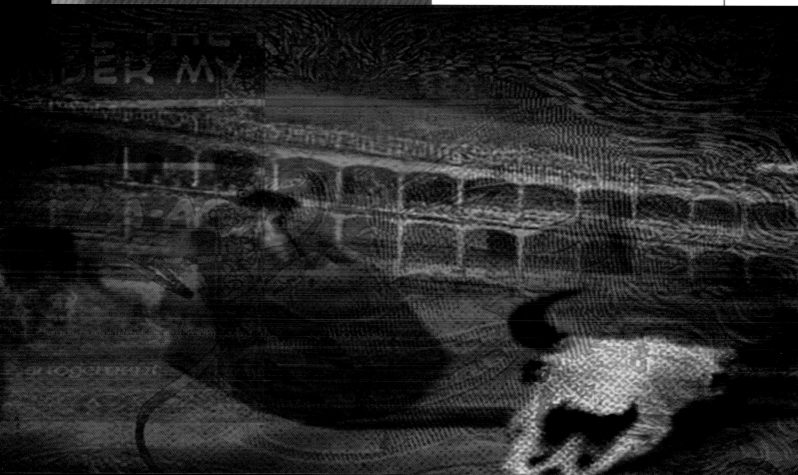

NDER MY

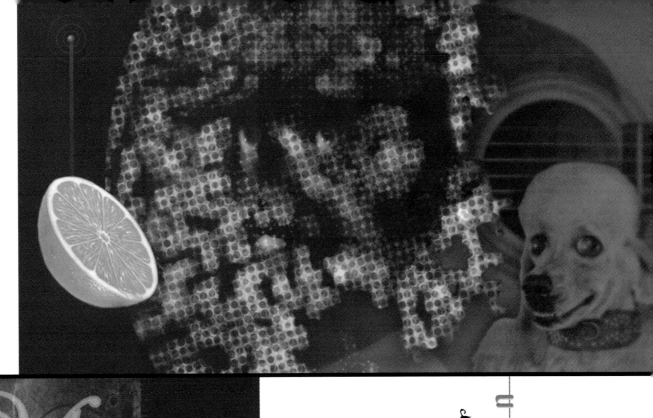

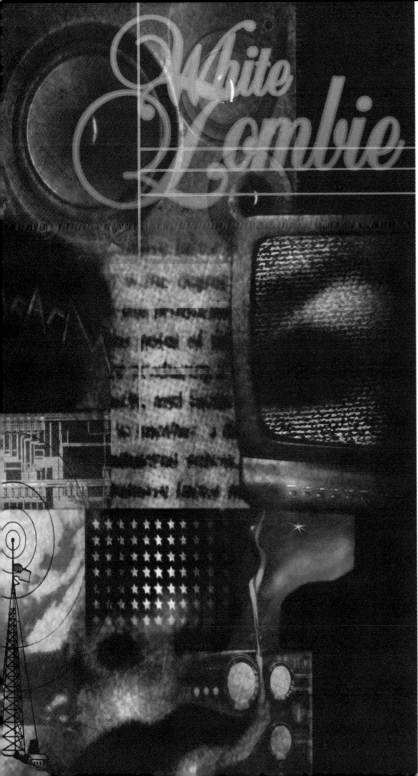

Concert poster

purpose

Paul watson

client

Folk Implosion

software

AdobePhotoshop

Folk Implosion

Concert poster

purpose

Paul watson

client

White Zombie

software

AdobePhotoshop

White Zombie

Band Advertisement

John J. Hill

digital creative

Seven2

client

Adobe Photoshop

software

Seven2

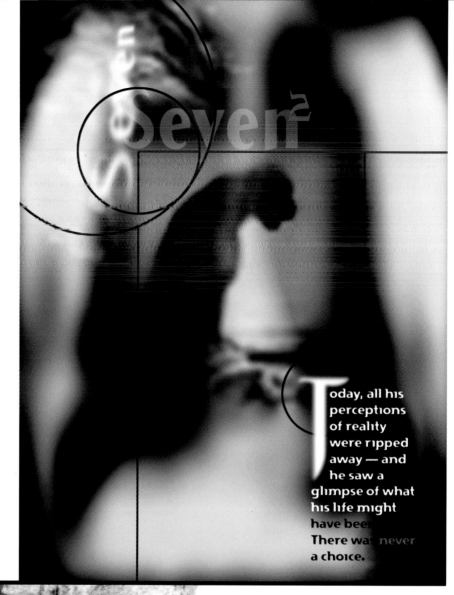

Today, all his perceptions of reality were ripped away — and he saw a glimpse of what his life might have been. There was never a choice.

digital creative

John J. Hill

client

Luminus Editions

Adobe Photoshop

software

Advertisement purpose

Luminus

Promotional Material

Ledge

digital creative

JohnJ.Hill

52mmine.

client

AdobePhotoshop

57

AdvertiSemenT

AD

purpose

digital creative

JohnJ.Hill

52mmine.

client

AdobePhotoshop

software

The **pulsating imagery** of Dale Graham's show reel ouch, for his media design

self **P**romotion purpose

**o u c h** S h o w R e e l

OUCh

the digital creative

client OUCh

Ado**be** Photoshop, Illustrator software

OUCh

agency, is methodically

premeditated **to tease**

the observer into **wanting more.** The

goal was to create a brief,

**The colorful melange**

**of images** shows how entertaining piece that

would showcase the

group's work and

**Graham and his** partner Vicky Lemont would **keep**

**viewers engaged**

**like to push** the limits of their art using Adobe Illustrator and Adobe Photoshop.

**Each visual bite is curious and flavorful enough** that the viewer

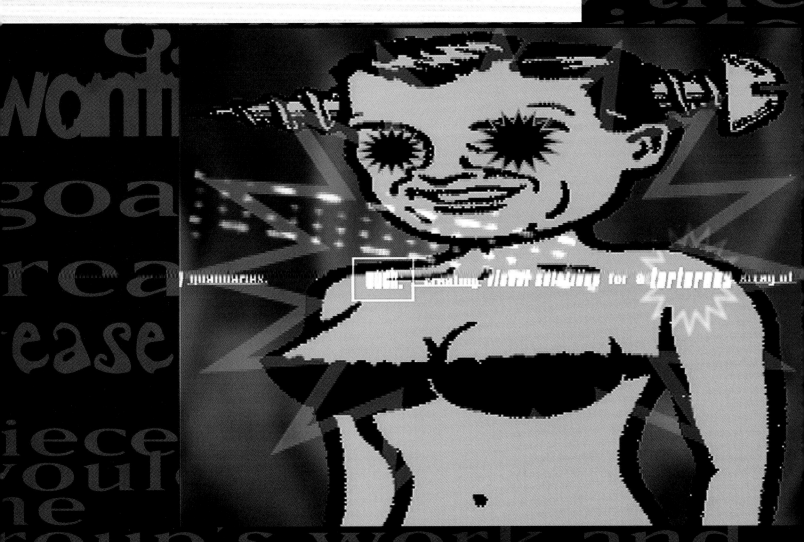

self Promotion
purpose

Revolver

Jeff Düingfelder, Sue Z Smith
digital creative

client
Studio DNA
client

Adobe Photoshop
software

WORLD'S BIGGEST REVOLVER

Disintegrating type and uncommon visuals propose a marriage of the **absurd** in **"Revolver,"** a **collabora-tive** design by Jeff Düngfelder and Sue Z Smith. In a *wry* juxtaposition of obsession with rationaliza-tion, **the world's largest revolver** is visually linked with a flasher, a gunslinger and **out-of-control** cars. The underlying text denies everything.

**Düngfelder and Smith** who created the work in Adobe Photoshop, say they enjoy pursuing a *skewed psychological* angle when they assemble images. Inspired by the social anomalies in an *absurd universe,* they like to **reach a viewer on many levels.**

# KISS

# Max

## month

# KISS

of
the

Mar
Apr

Promotion : purpose
Cinemax : Kiss of the Month

digital
creative
ouch

client
Cinemax
Mark
Davidson

software
Adobe
Photoshop

digital
creative
ouch

client
FinishEditorial! Don Packer

Brand Identity : purpose
finish Fire logo

software
Adobe
Photoshop
Illustrator

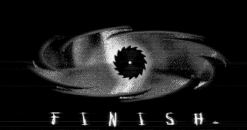

FINISH.

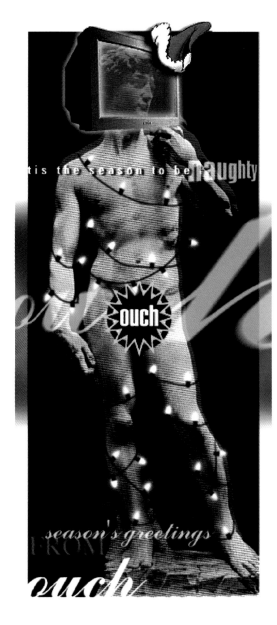

'tis the season to be naughty

ouch

season's greetings FROM

ouch

Holiday Card

**Holiday Card**

purpose
digital creative

ouch

client

ouch

software

Adobe
Photoshop
Illustrator

63

Unpublished

**Unpublished**

purpose

digital creative

ouch

client

ouch

software

Adobe
Photoshop

Matt CavE

digital creative

software

AdobePhotoshop

self Promotion

purpose

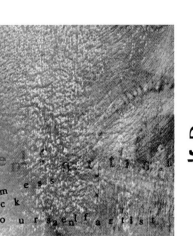

Artist Block2

The obsession of TV. The new religion.

purpose

TV - ism

Kip Henrie

digital creative

client

self Promotion

software

AdobePhotoshop, Illustrator

# butter

buffalo daughter

september 7, lee's palace

Concert poster
purpose

Butter

digital creative
PauL watson

client
Butter

software
AdobePhotoshop

Concert poster
purpose

Melvins

digital creative
PauL watson

client
MelvinS

software
AdobePhotoshop

# MELVINS
with L7

NoV 29
THE
WAREHOUSE

Concert poster
purpose

Polvo

PauL watson
digital creative

pOlvo
client

software
AdobePhotoshop

This rendering is part of a larger body of meditations o

Artist Lanny Quarles used digitized sculptural figures to con
**living interface** or browser for the sensual universe
The addition of real eyes and lips to the central figure bring
into a live one lost in t h o u

According to Quarles, the frame of the in

consciousness in the histo

Inside the ChemWindow application window:

ChemWindow - C:\CHE3WIND\XUP.CW2

File  Edit  Arrange  Options  Font  Size  Style  Other  Help

Drag=Create bezier

CHELIDONIA

Sch00611.jpg

Using Adobe Photoshop, Quarles takes samples from the web and composes spontaneously, without any forethought: "Experimentation is the mother of all virtue," he says. His illustrations evolve from found imagery and the artist's general precepts about the subject matter.

perception of reality.

his belief that the body is a kind of

life, and transforms a stone woman

h t .

becomes much like the famework of

field.

Experimental Study purpose

Cadmon

Lalny R. Quarles digital creative

software

Adobe Photoshop, Web Sampling

69

self Promotion purpose

Alien Nike

digital creative Design
LaX Syntax Design

software Adobe Photoshop

client LaX Syntax Design

70

In Adobe Photoshop, the Lance saved video stills as JPEGs, then **merged** and modified the composite image with color dodge-and-burn filters. The shoe was drawn and colorized in **Adobe Illustrator.** The figure appears to be in a **trance**-or it may be pulling the viewer under its power. The **hypnotic** effect of the circulating background pulls us in even further.

The overw helming, insidious "
the premise of Alien Nike, a huge
like yet steely emotionless is uncanny
A huge, fl oating athletic shoe in the
familiar wo rld  also creates a disorienting
ing VISUAL

The overwhelming, insidious "easternizatio
The main figure, human-like yet steely emotionles
A huge, floating athletic shoe in the background
creates a disorienting visual ten

VISUAL TENSION

views o

... of consumerism" is the premise of "Alien Nike," by Lance Jackson. Uncomfortably close to the viewer, l o o m i n g in a rather menacing way. piece of our more familiar world, but its scale and relationship to the alien ion. Jackson used four video stills to capture views of a Japanese toy.

Experimental **Study**

Boppl *purpose*

Lanny R. Quarles

*digital creative*

**A**dobe **P**hotoshop,

**F**ractal **P**oser,

**W**eb **S**ampling

72

Experimental **Study**

XXIA *purpose*

*digital creative*

Lanny R. Quarles

*software*

**A**dobe **P**hotoshop

Experimental Study

Cusanos

Lanny R. Quarles

Adobe Photoshop,
Web Sampling

Experimental Study

Kekule

Lanny R. Quarles

Adobe Photoshop

Lanny R. Quarles

Adobe Photoshop

Experimental Study

purpose

ukol

74

Magazine Editorial

purpose

Aurora web

LaX Syntax Design

Communications Week International

Adobe Photoshop

LaX Syntax Design

New Media ShoWcase

Adobe Photoshop

CoVer Art

NMS94

Lax Syntax Design

Self Promotion          Adobe Photoshop

Self Promotion

76

Greeting Card Series

Check The
Gene Pool

Lax Syntax Design

client

Urban Outfitters & Lax Syntax Design

Adobe Photoshop

LaX Syntax Design

Self Promotion

Adobe Photoshop

Self Promotion

Image Retention

77

Greeting Card Series

purpose

Arrested

Adolescence

LaX Syntax Design

client

Urban Outfitters & LaX Syntax Design

Adobe Photoshop

The SearCh in the **Lost SugaR FaCtory Series**

purpose

Rafael Peixoto Ferreira

digital creative

FractaL deSigN Painter, Adobe Photoshop, Convolver, Corel Draw software

pressure

Co-animation on an e

a organic aspect

A **cloud of energy** found in an
technology-is captured in Rafael Fer
collages based on an explor
*dark side* of technology and desig
of M I N D pressure.

Ferreira says the gods
and saints in his art
represent everyone's
imaginary fears. In the
background, a figure,
seemingly masked by
newer technology, looks
on suspiciously.
Ferreira doesn't try to
create an
impossible,unrealistic
utopia in his work. His
reservoir of new
concepts comes from
contemporary subcultures
and chaos in everyday
life.

**Video Loop**

purpose

**Movie 5**

**Ramina Khachi**
digital creative

software

**Adobe** Photoshop, After Effects

**Adaptec**

We move the info

Although information technology is the subject of the video, the organic colors and shapes used in the art create a comforting, non-threatening environment for the viewer. In fact, the movement and palette in the piece are a bit mesmerizing.

Artist Ramina Khachi wanted to get the tional video for Adaptec. Swirls of warm binary numbers move vertically and the and

Khachi worked in Adobe Photoshop and AfterEffects to design the illustration. The artist created her own evolving universe, a world in chaos, with an underlying super-structure of mathematical accuracy.

...t of speed, global uniformity, and movement in this promo-
...es, purples and greens suggest a high level of energy as the
...e circles. The word "extreme" appears after the numbers
...sphere are in motion.

**3Com Product**

purpose

P a c e

digital creative

Ramina Khachi

client

3Com Corporation

software

Adobe Photoshop, QuarkXpress

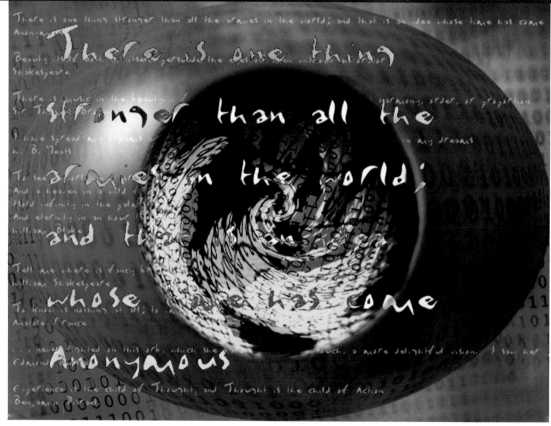

**Trade Show Video Loop**

purpose

Movie 2

digital creative

Ramina Khachi

client

Adaptec

software

Adobe Photoshop, After Effects

Morphic Poem

self Promotion

purpose

digital creative

Jeff Brice

software

Adobe Photoshop,
Adobe FreeHand

83

---

Brackets

self Promotion

purpose

digital creative

Jeff Brice

software

Adobe Photoshop,
Adobe FreeHand

---

presenting a surface which is being
perpetually renewed

RANDOMLY
FLUCTUATING
FIELDS

Mind

controlled operative force

influencing events in the

material world

working in the world without any guiding idea

Rafael Peixoto Ferreira

Fractal design Painter, Adobe Photoshop, Convolver, Corel Draw

The Search in the Lost Sugar Factory Series

R.P. Typewriter

TECHNOLOGY BROUGHT DEATH TO THE TYPEWRITERS

The Search in the Lost Sugar Factory Series

Bauhaus Nightmare

The 90s are the Bauhaus nightmare

I AM THE ONLY RUNNING FOOTMAN

Rafael Peixoto Ferreira

Fractal design Painter, Adobe Photoshop, Convolver, Corel Draw

Welcome to:
Rafael Peixoto
Ferreira
GRAPHIC
DESIGN
PAGE

n links, design culture, Brazil's D
d an e-mail to a nice conversation
country's Design.... I AM HERE to hea
rfdesign@dglnet.com.br

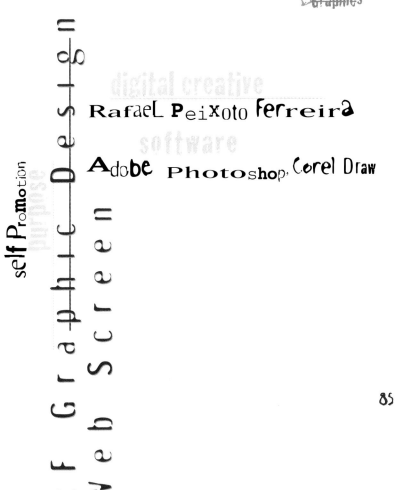

self Promotion
purpose

RF Graphic Design
Web Screen

digital creative
software

Rafael Peixoto Ferreira

Adobe Photoshop, Corel Draw

85

The Search in the Lost Sugar Factory Series
purpose

Living in
the Dust

digital creative
software

Rafael Peixoto Ferreira

Fractal design Painter,
Adobe Photoshop, Convolver, Corel Draw

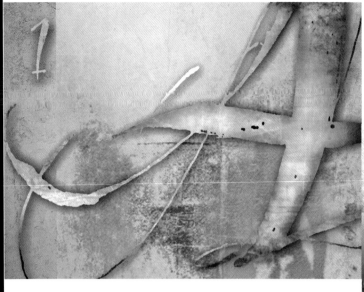

ProMotioNAL Cards

ABCD purpose

digital creative

John Ritter

client

Lilly Lee
Lettering DesiGN

software

Adobe Photoshop

*Hand Lettering Lilly Lee*

Article on Electronic Font Issues

Front Issue Update

digital creative

John Ritter

client

MacWoRld Magazine

software

Adobe
Photoshop

Promotion

Cinemax: What
Do They Do?

digital creative

ouch

client

Cinemax:
Andy Verderama

software

Adobe Photoshop,
Discreet Logic Flame,
Adobe AfteR Effects

master electrician    William Z. Hanley
best boy electric    Peter Tyzver
supervising electrician    Samuel K. Kryzinski
prop master    Steven Lee Beaudry
wardrobe supervisor    Bella Smitherton-Langly
assistant wardrobe supervisor    Dennis Flame
negative cutter    Zue Phan Yught
assistant negative cutter    Chi Ling Pho
film loader    Tommy Halston
vehicle services    Western Auto Supply of
Zak Tellington III
make-up supervisor    Monique De La Veronica
lead make-up artist    Kaleh Hernande Bellowson

Anastasia Vasilakis created this self promotional

work, but
the artist depends on the viewer's

**subCONSCIOUS** to complete the

thought.

Like a **f r a g m e n t** of silent movie film, three

frames tell an **incomplete** story.

Vasilakis tries to

**entice** the **internal sense**

of the audience to fill

in the blanks and coalesce the tale she began.

The computer is just one tool in the **artist's**

**p r o c e s s** : She uses Adobe Photoshop and

QuarkXPress to manipulate  scanned photos

and **saturate** their **colors**. She

prints out the results and then paints,

cuts up and re-scans them. At this moment, the

**digital process** begins **anew.**

self **Pro**m**o**tion

**B o y  S c o u t**

digital creativity

**Anastasia Vasilakis**

digital creative

Adobe Photoshop® **QuarkX**press

software

Vasilakis' choice of a friendly, familiar boy scout poster, and

several **l e s s  comforting** military-like images, sets the

**e**y**e** **in  mo**tion. The viewer senses the *Rhythm* and

associations in the art, but must **search** to find their meaning.

The messages in Cristina Casañas' lace-like art, titled Isis, are as layered as the images it contains. The artist used a circle to represent a **cipher**, and at th same time, life and the creative process. Isis, th *goddess of nature*, dwells within, representing motherhood and the **cyclical nature of life**. After further study, another impression is born from the background:

Are the uplifted hands those of an infant, as seen through ultrasound? Are the large masses the baby's developing body, **floating in amniotic** fluid? Then the circle is a womb, simultaneously framing the child and its mother in a true **circumference of life.** Casañas scans images, textures and objects into Adobe Photoshop, then repeatedly superimposes them to create a sense of depth in which the viewer can lose himself.

The artist says her goal is to create art tha

self ProMotion
purpose

isis

Cristina CaSAñaS
digital creative

software
Adobe Photoshop

not be disassembled and which offers no clue as to its construction.

Personal Print

purpose

Nina

digital creative

John Ritter

software

Adobe
Photoshop

ARTEMIS

self Promotion

purpose

Artemis

digital creative

Cristina CasAñas

AlterNative Pick
1998

client

Adobe Photoshop

software

self Promotion

purpose

Lotus Blossom

digital creative

Cristina CaSAñaS

software

Adobe Photoshop

Gallery Exhibition

purpose

June

digital creative

Cristina CaSAñaS

client

The Art INStitute of BOston

software

Adobe Photoshop

94

self P<sub>r</sub>o<sub>m</sub>otion
p u r p o s e
p l a y g r o u n d

digital creative
Anastasid Vasilakis

software
Adobe Photoshop,
QuarkXpress

self P<sub>r</sub>o<sub>m</sub>otion
purpose
s l e e p e r

digital creative
Anastasid Vasilakis

software
Adobe Photoshop,
QuarkXpress

**Editorial** *purpose*

**Survivors**

Anastasid Vasilakis *digital creative*

*client*

Rutgers Magazine

Adobe Photoshop, *software* QuarkXpress

95

**Editorial** *purpose*

**Survivors 2**

*digital creative*

Anastasid Vasilakis *client*

Rutgers Magazine

Adobe Photoshop, QuarkXpress *software*

INFUSED WITH THE ENERGY

GRIND

STOP MOTION

ROAST

CUPPA COFFEE
ANIMATION

416 340 8869

ENLIVEN SUGGESTING MOVEMENT

Advertising

purpose

Cuppa Coffee
Animation

digital creative

Anastasia Vasilakis

client

Cuppa Coffee
Animation

Adobe Photoshop

software

Editorial

purpose

Criminal

digital creative

Anastasia Vasilakis

client

The Washington Post

software

Adobe Photoshop,
QuarkXpress

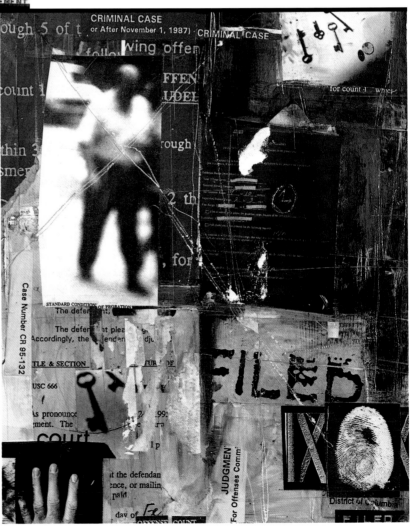

CRIMINAL CASE
or After November 1, 1987)  CRIMINAL CASE

ough 5 of t

follo wing offen

count 1

FFEN
UDEL

thin 3

rough

sme

2 th

, for

for count 1 whic

Case Number CR 95-132

STANDARD CONDITIONS OF PROBATION
The defendant,

The defen ant plea
Accordingly, the e endan dju

TLE & SECTION              UR DE

USC 666

as pronounce
ment. The

court

I p

FILED

IX

t the defendan
ence, or mailin
paid

day of

JUDGMEN
For Offenses Comm

District of Columbia

OFFENSE COURT            FILED

self Promotion

tango

digital creative

Anastasia Vasilakis

software

Adobe Photoshop, QuarkXpress

Mystery, impending enlightenment and peril are the central themes of this illustration, created by Ronald Dunlap of Doglight Studios, one in a series of eight images for a proposed book of fiction. Based on the premise of a tourist traveling in north Africa in the mid-1950s, the art uses as its focal point a seated statue of the Egyptian god Anubis.

Concept Visual

purpose

Anubis Note

digital creative

Ronald Dunlap

client client

Hieronymus Wittkamp Design

Adobe Photoshop

software

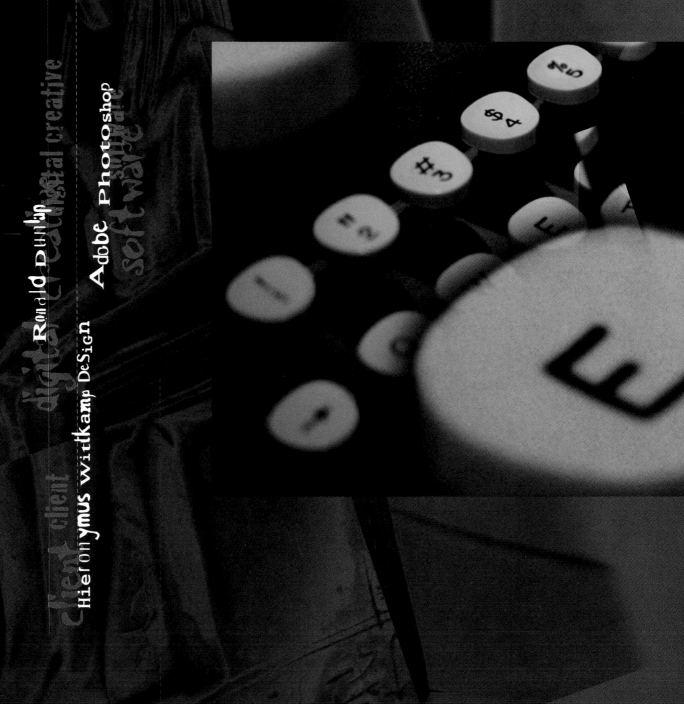

Lord of the Horizon, **Anubis** can see the world of life as well as the netherworld, where he guides the dead.

Dunlap included the typewriter to symbolize a means of systematic knowledge. Enamored by Egyptian metaphors and symbolism, his studio makes images as unaffected as possible, despite the fact some contain over thirty Adobe Photoshop layers. The artist says his layering techniques allow him to correct flaws in the original photograph while framing appealing, natural shapes.

Mark Allen
digital creative

software
Adobe Photoshop

The transformation from print to motion graphics, from flat, static lettering to living dimensional art was Mark Allen's goal in this intro screen to his website. Allen created the dimensional effect in Adobe Photoshop as a way of moving from still to moving image. The background is a melange of typography and photos shot by the artist.

The image features
repr
artist's specia

llen's logo, a stylized **M** and **A** united by a crossbar,
tative of a quill pen and hand-lettering, one of the
es.

Ronald Dunlap

Henry Brothers Studios

Adobe Photoshop

Ad BacKGround Illustration

purpose

Number 1

digital creative

client

software

self Promotion

purpose

Angel in Pool

Ronald Dunlap

client

Dooglight Studios

Adobe Photoshop

digital creative

software

CD Booklet Illustration

New Techo

digital creative
purpose

Ronald Dunlap

client

Hieronymus Wittkamp Design

software

Adobe Photoshop

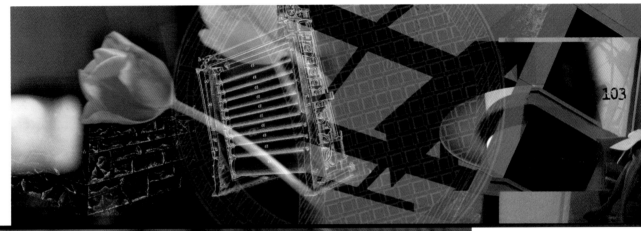

Poster Illustration
purpose

Kerli

digital creative

Ronald Dunlap

client

Big City

Adobe Photoshop

software

Mark Allen

Adobe Photoshop, QuarkXpress, Hand Lettering

digital creative

software

client Warner Brothers

MoVie Title

Sweet Nothing

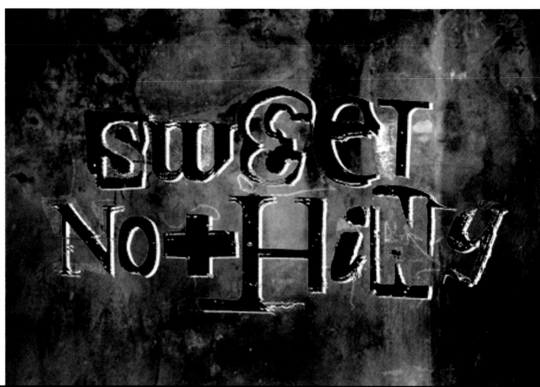

mark allen

pictures

Still Frame from Mark Allen's ReeL

purpose

Mark Allen

Pictures

digital creative

Mark Allen

software

Adobe Photoshop, Premier, After Effects

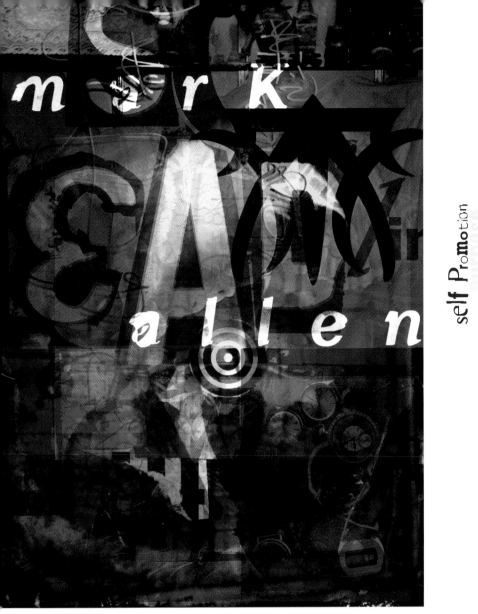

self Promotion

Mark Allen Postcard

Mark Allen

Adobe Photoshop,
QuarkXpress

digital creative

105

Mark Allen

Book on Marks Fine Art

Book Cover

Mark Allen

Adobe Photoshop,
QuarkXpress

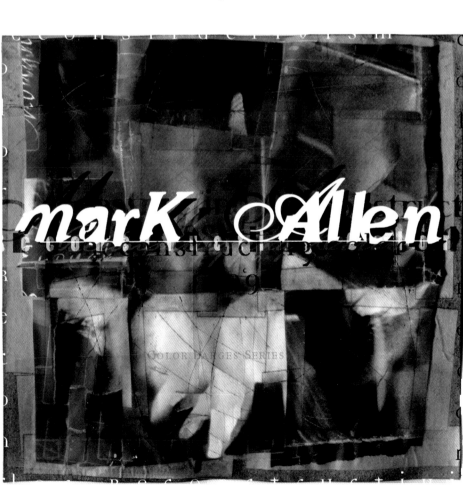

Web Site

396

Mark Allen

Adobe Photoshop

Logo & Stationery for Storm/Publishers of Alternative Pick

Storm Identity

purpose

digital creative

software

client

Mark Allen

Storm Music Entertainment, Inc.

Adobe Photoshop, QuarkXpress, Hand Lettering

Rafael Peixoto Ferreira

Anti-Materia design

Pixar Typestry, Adobe Photoshop, Corel Draw

self Promotion for Anti-Materia design

purpose

Anti-Materia (Inverted)

Anti-Materia

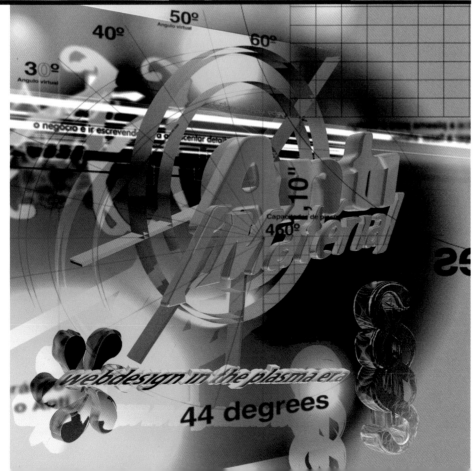

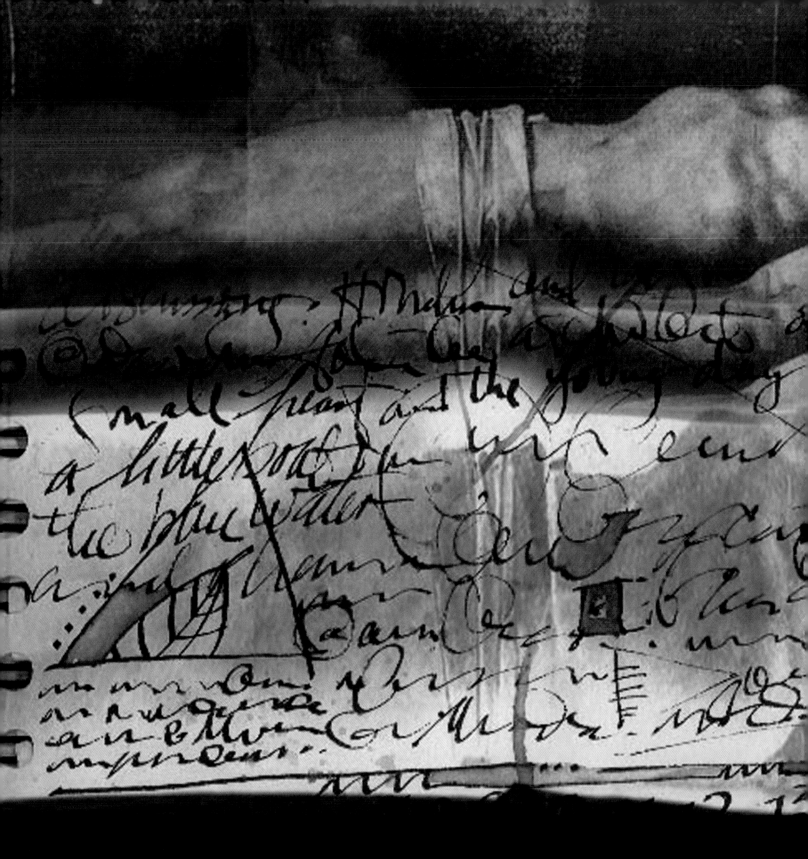

The structure of the work allows for several interpretations: Perhaps the written messages rep

**life flowing from the body**. Perhaps the words are

figuratively or literally. Perhaps the words are blanketing the body.

disappeared. Birchman allows his art to develop on its own. He begins with a kernel of an idea-i

of Christ-and starts combining images until they speak to each other in a narrative o

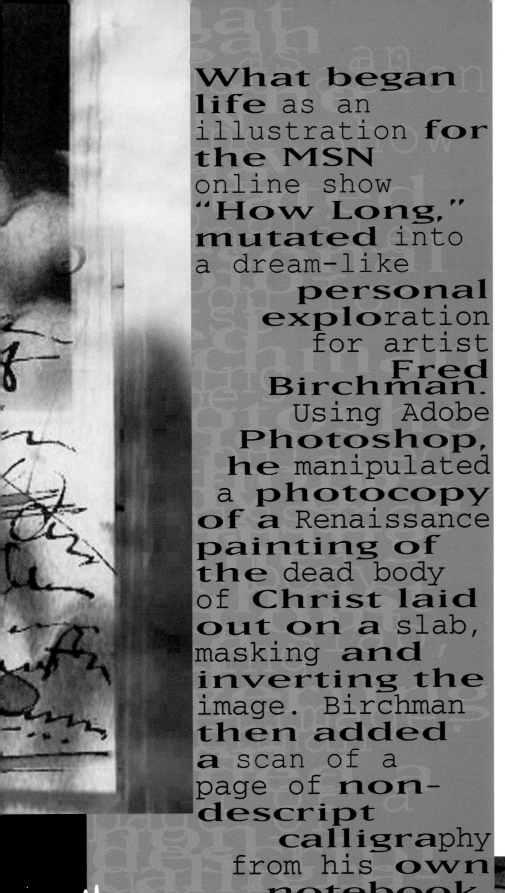

What began life as an illustration for the MSN online show "How Long," mutated into a dream-like personal exploration for artist **Fred Birchman**. Using Adobe Photoshop, he manipulated a **photocopy of a** Renaissance **painting of the** dead body **of Christ laid out on a** slab, masking **and inverting the** image. Birchman **then added a** scan of a page of **non-descript calligraphy** from his **own notebook. The** effect is a softly **colored,** slightly dimensional illuminated manuscript.

sing the person, after the physical remains have ase, the **metaphor** sthetic sense.

0nLine Illustration
purpose

software

Adobe Photoshop

FRed BiRchmAn
digital creative

francis

MSN/Self Promotion

client

109

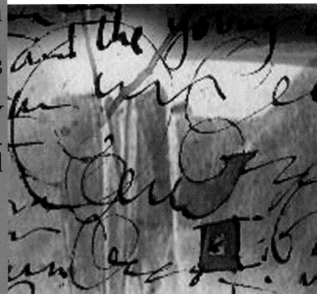

Self Promotion/Art Project

purpose

Ehrensvärd

Seppo K. Niiranen
digital creative

soft software
Adobe Photoshop

Niiranen rejected the crude randomness of his software and elected to work like a traditional artist who carefully planned

Niiranen rejected the
his software and elec
traditional artist w
the composition an
ings, ever aware of
will occur once the
touches the i
believes
the work i
by how v
ca
interactions
tools and th

Seppo Niiranen was intrigued by the randomness he created with "Ehrensvärd." one illustration in a 26-part alphabet of architectural images. entitled "Alphabets of Architecture." Each letter represents a famous Finnish architect.

Many things are hidden inside the image: an "e" for Ehrensvärd (a naval officer who designed military buildings), King's Gate; the fortress island of Suomenlinna and one of the oldest remaining buildings in Helsinki, a map, and an antique photo of military soldiers.

ide randomness of
to work like a
carefully planned
color of his paint-
e uncertainty that
ush
egular canvas. He
e quality of
determined
ll the artist
control the
etween the
medium.

self Promotion/Art Project
purpose
Wartiainen

digital creative

Seppo K. NiiRanen

Adobe software
Photoshop

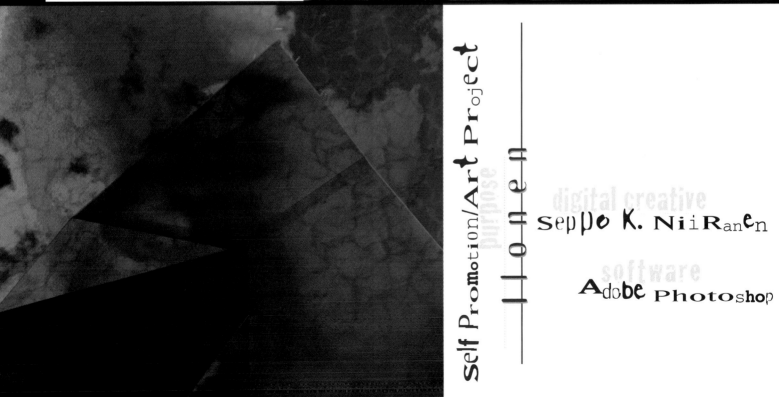

self Promotion/Art Project
purpose
Honen

digital creative

Seppo K. NiiRanen

software

Adobe Photoshop

Extreme Graphics

self Promotion/Art Project

purpose

Aalto

digital creative

Seppo K. NiiRanen

software

Adobe Photoshop

self Promotion/Art Project

purpose

Välikangas

digital creative

Seppo K. NiiRanen

software

Adobe Photoshop

purpose **Nyström**

self **Promotion/Art Project**

digital creative

**seppo K. NiiRanen**

**A**dobe **Photoshop** software

purpose **Ruusuvuori**

self **Promotion/Art Project**

digital creative

**seppo K. NiiRanen**

software

**A**dobe **Photoshop**

Self Promotion/Art Project

ullberg

digital creative

sep[Jo K. NiiRanen

software

Adobe
Photoshop

digital creative

# FRed BiRchmAn

client

MSN

software

**A**do**be** Photoshop

Illustration/0ɴLine Show

plum

purpose

digital creative

# FRed BiRchmAn

software

**A**do**be**
Photoshop

Portfolio

purpose

wire

TRAGEDIE

1948

software

**A**do**be P**hoto**shop**

**P**ortfolio

Soul purpose

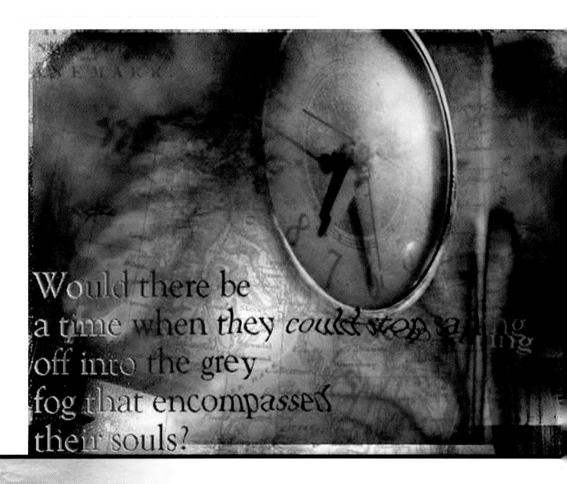

Would there be
a time when they could stop falling
off into the grey
fog that encompassed
their souls?

180°

75°

165°

digital creative

FRed BiRchmAn

software

**A**do**be P**hoto**shop**

**P**ortfolio purpose

Western

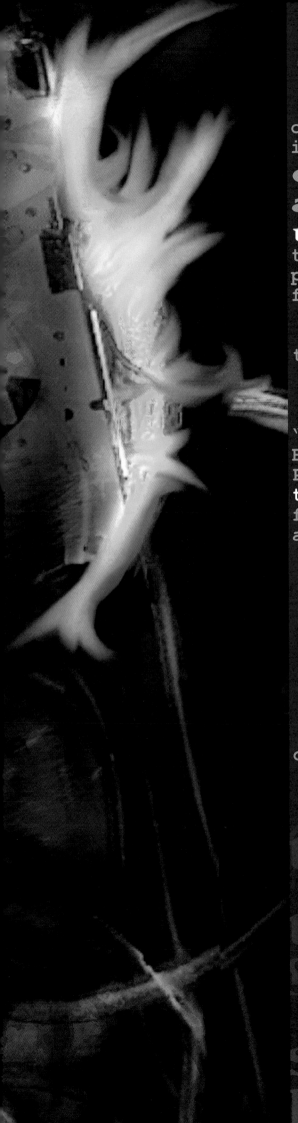

This was artist Troy Bennett's premise for **Catboy**, part of an investigation into the **digitization and manipulation** of the evolutionary process. A cat's face, with eyes like flickering screens, is **superimposed** on the **head of a child.** The creature's glare is confrontational, as if to ask, "Who has the right?" Bennett used Abobe Photoshop to create the **disturbing** face and adds wires and other electronic circuitry to complete the image. The artist graphically shows how the blending of **genetics**, media and technology could dramatically affect our everyday lives in the future or perhaps it already has.

As scientists untangle and learn how to **manipulate genetics**, the possibility of strange, **hybrid** creatures becomes less of a subject for science fiction and more of a **REALITY.**

self Promotion purpose

C a t b o y

digital creative Troy Bennett

Adobe Photoshop software

Personal Piece
purpose
Pandora's Box

digital creative
Michael Morgenstern
digital creative

software
software
Adobe Photoshop

Morgenstern likes the enigmatic

effects he can create in Adobe

Photoshop by mixing such

fragments

into new, organic forms

that still radiate something

of their original intent.

"The viewer's eye is com-

pelled to move," he says,

"continually forming new

meanings and relationships

between the parts."

There is an

ethereal effect

of movement

within the frame.

In this wor

we ca

Pa

ist Michael Morgenstern wanted to illustrate the idea that there are doors

not open without upsetting an essential

balance in nature, either on a personal or grand-scale level.

a's Box is constructed in Adobe Photoshop from different sources which alchemize

together in a mysterious way.

Michael MorgeNstern

Adobe Photoshop

Personal Piece
fear
purpose

digital creative
software

Personal Piece
purpose
Ritual

Michael MorgeNstern

Adobe Photoshop

digital creative
software

CD Cover

purpose

digital creative

Michael MorgeNStern

client

Arpod MusiC, Inc.

software

Adobe Photoshop

All the Things We Cannot Know

B. RO

all the things we cannot know

Personal Piece

purpose

digital creative

Michael MorgeNStern

software

Adobe Photoshop

Beach Scene

Calendar Art

Freud Cyclops

digital creative

LaX Syntax Design

client

LaX Syntax Design

software

Adobe Photoshop

LaX Syntax Design

digital creative

PC World

client

Adobe Photoshop

software

Magazine Editorial

purpose

Celestial Child

Illustration for Yearly Report

Alderface

purpose

digital creative

Seppo K. Niiranen

client

Finnish Cancer Organizations

software

Adobe Photoshop

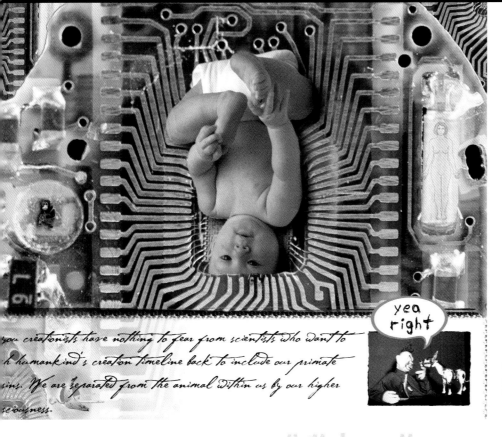

you creationists have nothing to fear from scientists who want to
h humankind's creation timeline back to include our primate
sins. We are separated from the animal within us by our higher
sciousness.

yea
right

self Promotion

purpose

yea Right

digital creative

Jeff Düngfelder, Sue Z Smith

client

Studio DNA

Adobe Photoshop

software

Michael MorgeNstern

Adobe Photoshop

digital creative

software

purpose

Personal Piece

Healer

Personal Piece

purpose

Millennium

digital creative

Michael MorgeNstern

software

Adobe Photoshop

Personal Piece

Enchantment

Michael MorgeNStern

Adobe Photoshop

Personal Piece

Blues Transformation

Michael MorgeNStern

Adobe Photoshop

The result is a powerful image
design elements rather than ele
organic materials s

Inspired by the iconography of Gothic and Flemish painting, Alessandro Bavari is a **painter** at heart. His early influences were van Eyck, Piero della Francesca and Paolo Uccello. He feels his strong traditional background in painting, photography and design afford him the creative foundation necessary to create innovative digital imagery.

This powerful extension of his traditional work, gives Bavari more control of his **com-plex** artwork.

After sketching the composition in pencil, Bavari takes black and white photographs, then experiments with acids, paints or **scratches on the prints**.

The photos are then scanned into Adobe Photoshop and recolored. He prefers combining images with organic materials such as fossils, bones or tar.

t relies on the sensitivity of the onic means to affect the viewer.

h as fossils.

Video Pr**é**sentation

purpose

D-e-m-e-t-r-a

Alessandro
digital creative Bavari

client Direct 2 Brain

software
Adobe Photoshop

dinYer

work, who he

his subject's rich, complicated inner life emanate from his paintin

quest is to

convey the same fleeti

soul's spiritual journey, rushing through the

tunnel of life, is the subject of **NearDeath**,

an illustration by Eric Dinyer created

for a U.S. News & World Report on

near death experiences.

**The central figure is** pulled

away from the viewer and the

world into a **mysteri-ous swirl** of light

and texture. The effect is at

the same time **gentle** yet **powerful**.

Eric Dinyer was an early and talented

newcomer to Adobe Photoshop for illustra-

He is inspired by **Rembrandt's**

ves is one of the few artists capable of letting

Dinyer's artistic

emotive quality in his work.

IllustRatioN
purpose
Near Death
digital creative
software
digital artist eric dinyer
Adobe Photoshop
US News & WoRLd RepoRt
client
crew

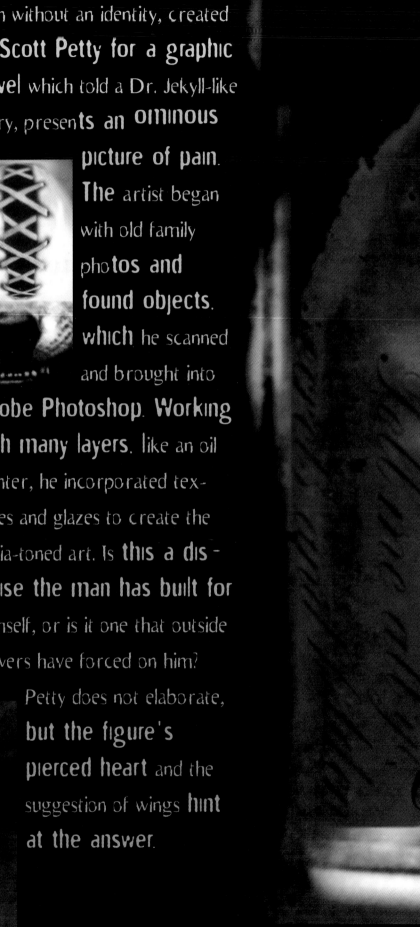

Graphic Novel **C**over
purpose

**Heart of a Madman**

**S**cott w. Petty digital creative
software **A**dobe Photoshop, **A**dobe Illustrator

client
**B**ee **H**ive **D**esign

This **haunting image** of a man without an identity, created by **Scott Petty** for a graphic **novel** which told a Dr. Jekyll-like story, presents an **ominous picture of pain.** **The** artist began with old family pho**tos and found objects.** **which** he scanned and brought into **Adobe Photoshop. Working with many layers.** like an oil painter, he incorporated textures and glazes to create the sepia-toned art. Is **this a disguise the man has built for** himself, or is it one that outside powers have forced on him? Petty does not elaborate, **but the figure's pierced heart** and the suggestion of wings **hint at the answer.**

The figure's vision is obscured by a **horrible** mask that seems to

ce its very skull: the rest of his face is hidden by a canine-like grin.

Eric **dinyeR**

**Dreamless** sTudioS

Adobe Photoshop

digital creative

client

software

face    purpose

self Promotion

purpose    fortress

Eric **dinyeR**

digital creative

Adobe Photoshop

software

IllusRate Divorce

Marriage

digital creative

Eric dinyeR

client

AnchoRAge Daily News

software

Adobe Photoshop

Editorial

Singapore Tiger

purpose

digital creative

Anastasia Vasilakis

client

Bloomberg Magazine

software

Adobe Photoshop
QuarkXpress

digital creative

Eric dinyer

CD Package

RCa RecordS

client

software

Adobe Photoshop

Lohengrin

Poetry Book IllustRatioN

digital creative

Eric dinyer

client

Luminaria

software

Adobe Photoshop

You Sing Aching

Purpose PaPeRPromotion

Time

digital creative
Scott FerguSon
client
WAuSAu PaPeRs
MARAthonCommuNicatiOns

software
Adobe Photoshop,
LiVe Picture

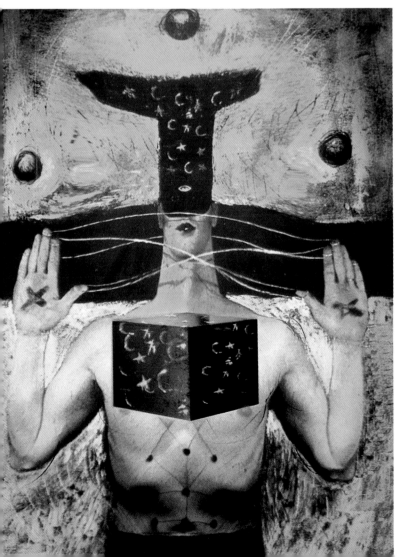

CD PackAge

Purpose

Black Box

digital creative
Eric dinyeR
client
TVT WaXtraX RecordS
software
Adobe Photoshop

digital creative

Eric dinyer

Adobe Photoshop

software

EnviRonmeNtal Book IllustRatioN

purpose

Gas Mask

138

self PRomotion

purpose

Il Riposo di Dafne
ed Artemide

digital creative

Alessandro
Bavari

software

Adobe Photosho

Invitation

purpose

Gluttony

digital creative

client

Scott Ferguson

DMB&B/St LouiS/AAAA

Adobe Photoshop, Metaflo

software

John Ritter

digital creative

Adobe Photoshop

software

Personal Piece

purpose

Lovers

In the final phase of human evolution

the technological externalisation of human

consciousness will become complete and the

net of this post human understanding will

be a ubiquitous global intelligence which

will entertain a scope of philosophical inquiry

beyond imagination.

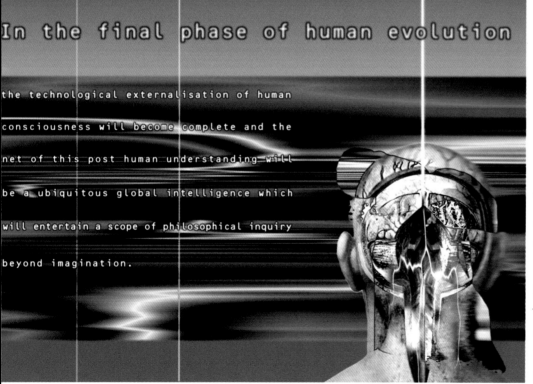

Peter Gudynas

digital creative

Adobe Photoshop

software

Fax Art Exhibition

purpose

Technocerebral

Eric dinyer

Luminaria

Adobe
Photoshop

Poetry Book IllustratioN

Rome

John Ritter

Jason Ingram Band.
Audience Records

Adobe Photoshop

Part of CD Package

Entredite

**P**ersonal **Pi**ece

purpose

Pulse Ritter

John **R**itter

digital creative

software

**A**dobe **P**hotoshop

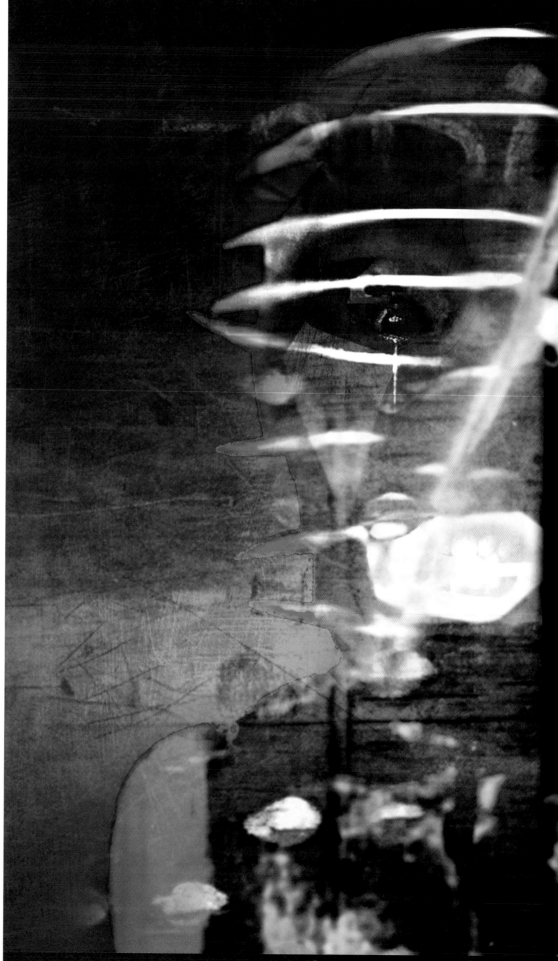

Ritter used Adobe Photoshop to combine his
image was created through spontaneous ex
the subject. The face of the helpless inmat
beyond the p o i n t o f s

A visit to the oldest prison in the United States, Eastern State Penn, spawned this disturbing image by John Ritter. The artist shot interior and exterior photographs to communicate the **effects of Quak**er rehabilitation techniques in the 1700s. Inmates were held in solitary confinement for three years with only a Bible and a small window for light. Many prisoners became emotionally **d i s t u r b e d** while incarcerated.

...tographs, sketches and acrylic painting on wood. The final ...rimentation to preserve the highly emotional nature of ...s a **haunting portrait** of the living dead, punished ...nity.

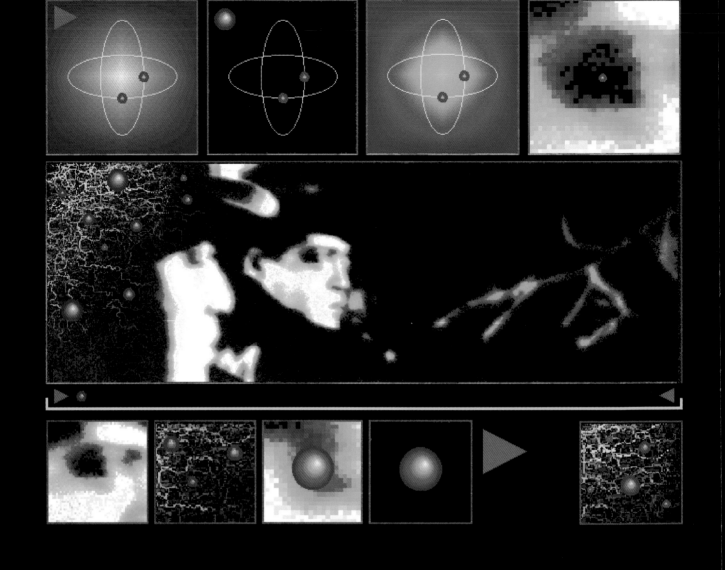

The cyberscape, created with 2d Designer Paint, explains

process: Electro-neural icon transmitt**ers are** implant

and **facilitate total**, direct interactiv

glowing orbs of colored ligh**t emerge from blackness**, cr

turns the **viewer's brain** in on itself.

Peter Gudynas insists that viewers of his multimedia presentation, Interneural, get inside of his main character-literally through the exploration of a technoir B movie inter cyber-space. Users of the presentation are granted "interneur-al access" that is, the ability to navigate within a dataspace environ-ment as represented by the simulated nervous system of the actor Peter Lorre.

nt X Corps incredible INTERNEURAL directly into the brain's cortex immersion. Flashes and ng a graphical representation that

Still Frame for a Multi-Media Presentation
purpose

Interneural

Peter Gudynas
digital creative

client
X Corps, F. Lang Simulations

2D Designer, software Paint, 8 bit Pluto Computer Graphics Controller

Cubanito

Editorial Illustration

**purpose**

Cristina CasAñaS

**client**

Rodm Magazine

**software**

Adobe Photoshop

digital creative

Let your beauty fly high
I'll clip your wings
Make you mine
Enslave the treasures and gifts
bestowed upon you
Decorate you in shimmering gold
and silver silk threads
Lace your mental with
thoughts of excruciating pain
Obsess you with my
domineering love
Make you think you want me more
than God
I'll empty your heart of
compassion
Substitute understanding
with hatred for humankind
~Joselyn Mirabal
XXQC

Left Eye of Horus

Exhibited in Realm of the Senses

**purpose**

digital creative

Cristina CasAñaS

**client**

Ward-Nasso Gallery

Adobe Photoshop

software

Cristina CaSAñaS

EMpire Records

Adobe Photoshop

digital creative
client
software
purpose
cd Art
RE

digital creative
client
software
purpose

FRed BiRchmAn

SalmoN STudioS

Adobe Photoshop

Web Site Project
Portal

Editorial

purpose

Crow

Anastasia Vasilakis

digital creative

Guitarworld Magazine

client

software

Adobe Photoshop,
QuarkXpress

rock

rock

self Promotion

purpose

jackedonnic

digital creative

Eric dinyer

software

Adobe Photoshop

Part of a **Video Installation** purpose

# Gasoline Study #1

digital
creative
software

John **R**itter

**A**dobe
**Photo**shop

digital creative

John **R**itter

software

**A**dobe **Photo**shop

**P**ersonal **P**iece purpose

# Paper Wire

**P**ersonal **study**

purpose

**A**eon

digital creative

**J**ohn **J**. **H**ill

**A**dobe software

**P**hoto**shop**

150

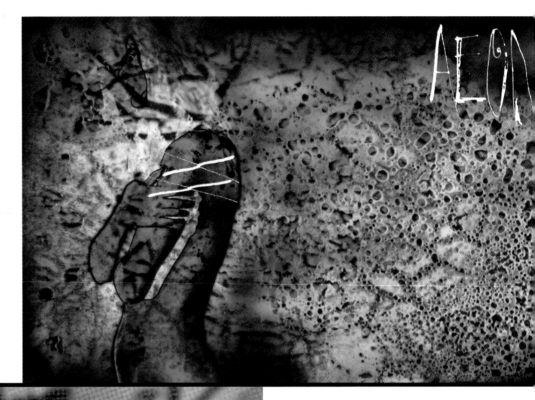

AEON

digital creative

**G**reg **P**as**c**o**S**

self **P**ro**m**otion

**A**dobe software

**P**hotoshop

purpose

**T**orso

Cristina Casañas

EMpire Records

Adobe Photoshop

Dancing Hathor

CD Art

purpose

Private Collection

Blu

purpose

digital creative

client

software

Cristina Casañas

Private Sale

Adobe Photoshop

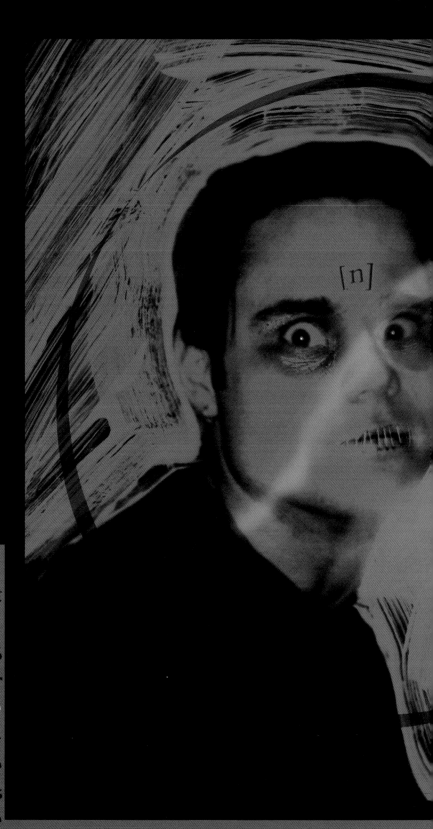

The struggle between good and
light an
emerge in "Julius and Nigel,"
begins with a very simple
with the multi-coloration
television, magazines an
color palette gives the eye a
work flows out of spontaneou
art ju

self Promotion
purpose
Julius & Nigel
digital creative
Matt cavE
Adobe Photoshop
software

152

[n]

For this piece, the artist painted **directly on a self** portrait photo for texture, then added tension by **viciously scratching** the eyes and lips with **a razor blade. He also** ripped the eyes of a baby from an early collage and scanned that image **together with his** self portrait into Adobe Photoshop for assembly and color manipulation. He used Adobe Illustrator to des

1, positive and negative,
dark, the inner child and the inner critic all
eerie photo-collage by Matt **Cave**. The artist
t strong palette. Most of his work contrasts
everyday life, with its confusing babble of
the Internet. According to Cave, the limited
lace to rest. Because he feels his best
play and experimentation, Cave lets **the**
happen without too much conscious planning.

ype and other graphic elements to portray the internal struggle between opposing forces.

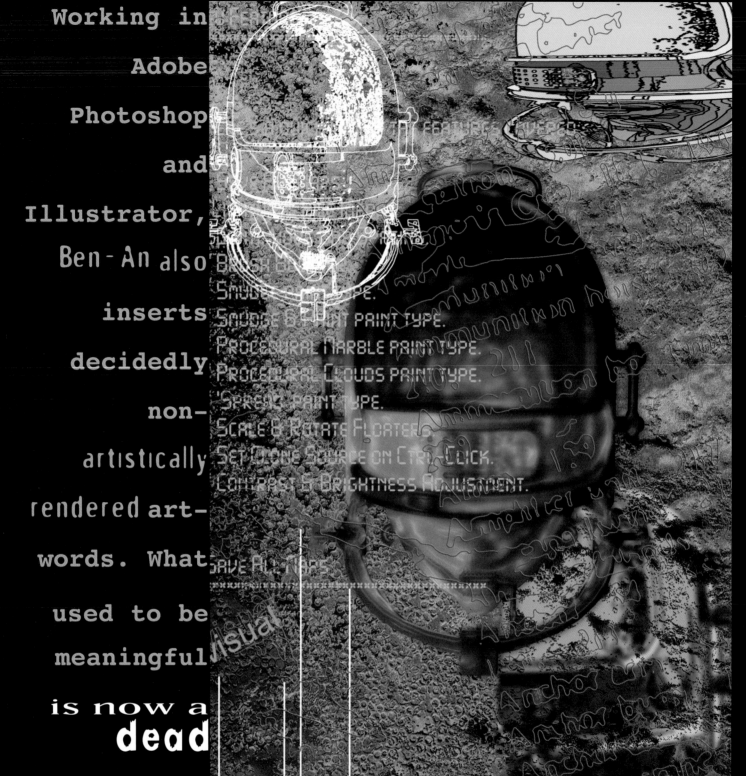

Working in Adobe Photoshop and Illustrator, Ben-An also inserts decidedly non-artistically rendered art-words. What used to be meaningful

is now a **dead** computer print-out. It is as if all humanity **has left the world, made cold and harshly** digital by **mankind's** indifference to **what was beautiful in life.**

In "2025" Ben-An makes a poignant statement about what life would be like after a nuclear ~~bomb~~ in the year 2025. Isolation and desolation are symbolized by the futuristic helmet. Empty helmets represent those who have been sacrificed in strife.

Advertising purpose
2025
Ben-An
digital creative

TTS Co., Ltd.
client

Adobe Photoshop Illustrator Lightwave
software

Ramina Khachi
Network Generals

Brochure Cover
purpose
Clock

Adobe Photoshop

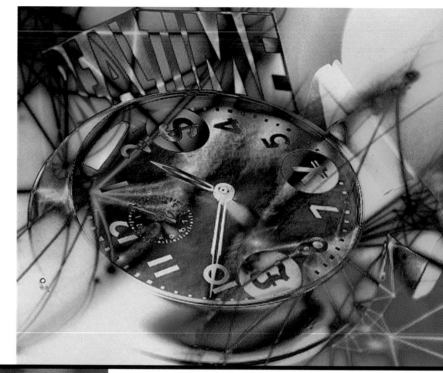

Trade Show/Leadership in Networking
purpose
Runner

Ramina Khachi

Network Generals

Adobe
Photoshop

digital
creative

Ramina
Khachi

client

Network
Generals

software

Adobe
Photoshop

Trade Show/Leadership in Networking

purpose

Network

Trade Show/Leadership in Networking

purpose

Bike

digital creative

Ramina Khachi

Network Generals

client

Adobe Photoshop

software

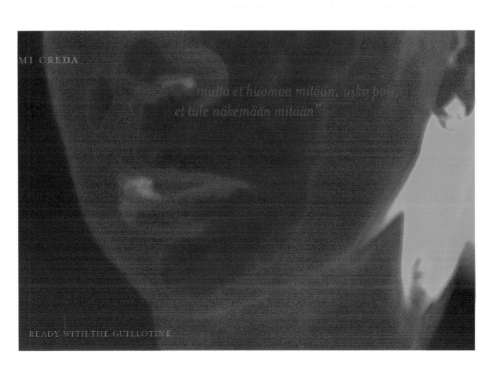

SELVÄSTIKIN JOS OTTAA KAIKEN KIRJAIMELLISESTI,

THERE ARE NO RULES OF BEHAVIOR

Käyttäytymiselle ei ole SÄÄNTÖJÄ
EHDOTTOMASTI

MI CREDA

mutta et huomaa mitään, usko pois,
et tule näkemään mitään"

READY WITH THE GUILLOTINE

SepPo K. NiiRanen

Adobe Photoshop
Macromedia Director

digital creative
software

International Collaborative Online Art Project

purpose

Passage Series

PromotioNal SponsorEd by Magazine

purpose

Absolut Absolution

digital creative

LaX Syntax DesIgn

client

FRisCO Magazine

software

Adobe Photoshop

Tony Schanuel

digital creative

New Warrior Network

Calendar

purpose

Quantum Mystic

client

Live Picture,
Adobe Photoshop

software

# dnd
## computers

On November 11, 1994,
Leonard Adleman published
a paper in Science[1]
describing the "Molecular
Computation of Solutions of
Combinatorial Problems".

This was the first ever implementation of a DNA-based
computer. Since then, many advancements have been
proposed to refine the protocol for programming a DNA
computer to reduce the complexity of the operations and
eliminate errors. [2,3] Despite their respective
complexities, biological and mathematical operations have
some similarities.

• The very complex structure of a living being is
the result of applying simple operations to initial
information encoded in a DNA sequence.

• The result (w) of applying a computable function
to an argument can be obtained by applying a
combination of basic simple functions to w.

• For the same reasons that DNA was presumably
selected for living organisms as a genetic material,
its stability and predictability in reactions, DNA
strings can also be used to encode information for
mathematical systems.

digital creative

Jeff Dillgfelder

Studio DNA

client

Adobe Photoshop,
Pixar Typestry

software

Self Promotion

purpose

DNA Computers

digital creative

Lisa A. Johnston

**A**dobe **P**hoto**shop**, **F**ractal **P**oser

software

self **P**romotion
purpose

**F**ield **F**igures

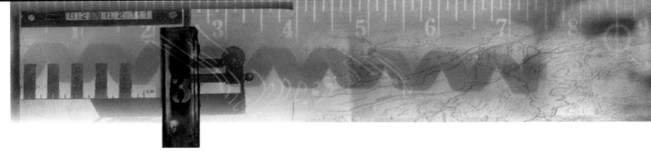

Web site **P**roject
purpose

**A**uger

digital creative

**FR**ed **B**i**R**chm**A**n

client

**S**almo**N S**tudio**S**

**A**dobe
**P**hoto**shop**

software

Mark Allen

Adobe Photoshop

Fine Art

Honey Bear with Frame

Mark Allen

Adobe Photoshop

Fine Art

Pave Rustment with Electric Chair

Ben-An

TTS Co., Ltd.

Adobe Photoshop
Illustrator,
Lightwave

Advertising

digital creative

client

purpose

software

Ben-An

ExtremE
Graphics

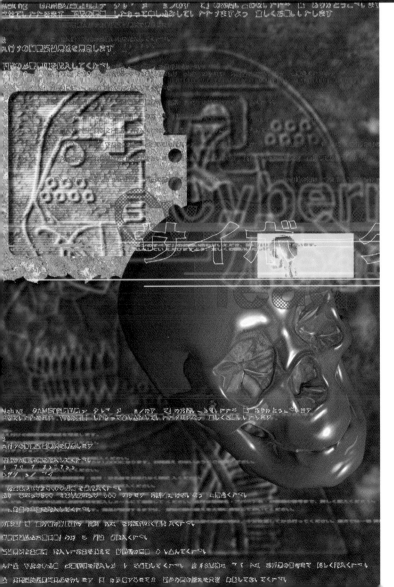

Ben-An

TTS Co., Ltd.

Adobe Photoshop
Illustrator,
Lightwave

digital creative

client

purpose

software

Advertising

Network

AGFA Type Specimen Book

Stephen Farrell
digital creative

purpose

Apologia

digital creative

Daniel X. O'Neil
writer
writer

software
Adobe Illustrator, Photoshop
software

+ I

+ 0

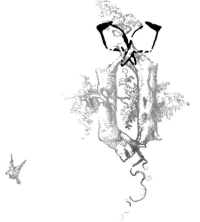

As in drama, we

are concerned not only with

what a character says, the lin-

guistic meanings and flavors

Each time we map a tornado, we attempt to master it to fit into a human

of the words, but with what

paradigm. The mapping structures give a picture of nature that is rational.

a character does with his

predictable, neutralized... AGFA commissioned this piece for a type

words. And around his

specimen book of both traditional and contemporary typefaces. Like a

words. The design

tornado, new typography has swept unpredictable patterns through the

articulates this subtext.

page landscape, challenging linearity and the orthodoxy of letterforms as a

transparent container. All this while feeding our freshly-laid type fetishes.

04/25/94
EL.00.6-
230KM
NR0
#4

· A

moist

unstable

SOME OF THAT CAKE.

ANTED TO COME OVER **TALK**: HAVE

PRECIPITATION CURTAIN

TORNADO

IN THERE ARE PRISONS

IN THE PATHS OF THESE

TURNADOES

PRESSURE
1012

excerpts from « *Apologia* », a poem by **Daniel X. O'Neil**   design by **Stephen Farrell**

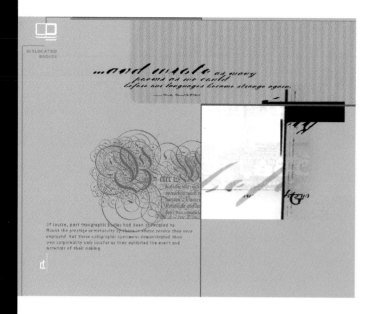

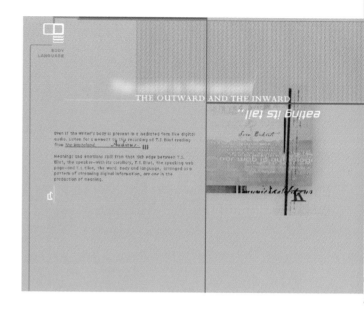

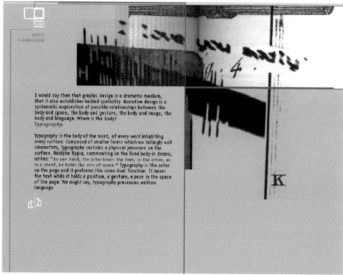

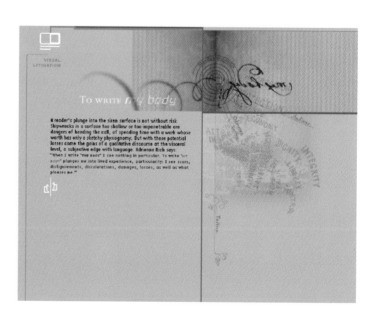

digital creative

**Stephen Farrell**

**Stephen Farrell**

writer

**Adobe Photoshop**

software

Web Essay

Body Language Impulse

Paper Theater

everlasting *like her tattoo* *virginity don't know its own name do you* *need for self definition* gin

167

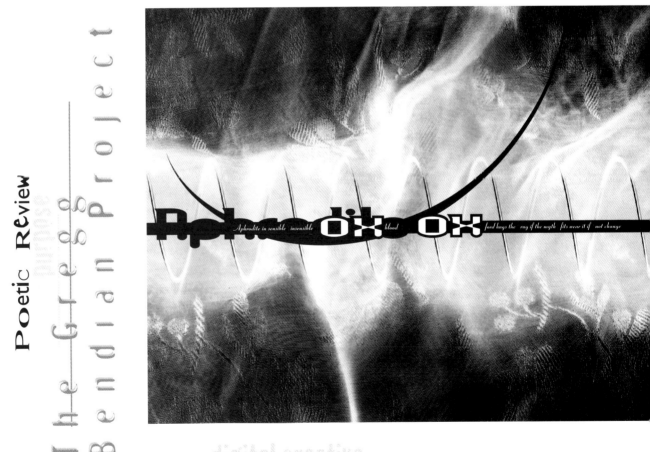

Poetic Review

The Gregg Bendian Project

*Aphrodite in sensible insensible blood ford hugs the rug if the myth fits wear it if not change*

Stephen Farrell

Brooke Bergan

Adobe Illustrator,

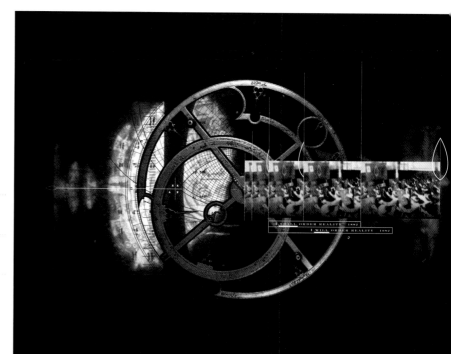

digital creative
Stephen Farrell

writer
Steve Tomasula

software
Adobe Illustrator, Photoshop

Experimental Fiction

TOC

purpose

everything is not yet here

THINGS START LIKE THIS. A LIFE
STARTS LIKE THIS. OUR PERSONALITY BEGINS WHEN WE REMEMBER
MOVE OURSELVES AND ENDS AHEAD OF US WILLING TO GET OMITTER AND
MOVE AROUND. RIPEN. NO CONTRADICTION CONTAINING AN OPPOSITE.

we're going too last, 0, be my reader, reader, author, eater
sniffing around, we need to keep a sense of proportion, forever
riding things Dorothy has a Dick after all, puts (or ancestors put)
together the abbreviated pictures of reconstruction. the idea like
a video store

yourself direct in profound abundance. you bury

Forward in Literary Arts Journal

purpose

A House Swarming!

Stephen Farrell

writer

D.R.Heiniger

software

Adobe Illustrator, Photoshop, Streamline

169

**BRONZE IRON PAPER**

*Sculpture Dervella Mcnee*

Stephen FaRReLL

digital creative

ArtiSt's LiaSon ATC GalleRy

client

Adobe IllustratoR,

software

Gallery Card
purpose

Bronze Iron & Paper

# Artist's Directory Index

### Domenic Ali
2594 Milvia
Berkeley, CA 94704
**Phone** 510-841-4218
**Email** dali@ziplink.net
**Website** http://www.ziplink.net/~dali/art
**p.**28, 32, 33, 34

### Mark Allen
Mark Allen Design
660 Venice Blvd./Suite 102
Venice, CA 90291
**Phone** 310-396-6471/212-243-4508
**Fax** 310-306-6834
**Email** mallendesign@earthlink.net
**Website** http://www.markallendesign.com
**p.**100, 104, 105, 106, 162

### Alessandro Bavari
Via Carducci 7
Latina, 04100 Italy
**Email** abArt@mbnet.it
**Website** http://www.bmnet.it/dedalo/
**p.**14, 15, 32, 34, 35, 37, 128, 138

### Troy Bennett
The Metaphysical Frontier Alliance
2046 #4 Monroe Avenue
Rochester, NY 14618
**Phone** 716-473-3442
**Email** troyb@art.net
**Website** http://www.art.net./~troyb
**p.**118

### Fred Birchman
2561 East Madison
Seattle, WA 98112
**Phone** 206-325-8312
**Email** fredb@wolfenet.com
**p.**108, 116, 117, 147, 161

### Jeff Brice
4510 171 Avenue S.E.
Snohomish, WA 98290
**Email** jb@jeffbrice.com
**Website** http://www.jeffbrice.com
**p.**10, 12, 13, 52, 53, 83

### Cristina Casañas
XQ Studios
779 Riverside Drive/#B12
New York, NY 10032
**Phone** 212-927-9037
**Fax** 212-927-9037
**Email** xqcasanas@xqc.com
**Website** http://www.xqc.com
**p.**90, 92, 93, 146, 147, 151

### Matt Cave
Cave Images
4967 SW 32 Way
Fort Lauderdale, FL 33312
**Phone** 954-893-7266
**Fax** 954-989-1670
**Email** matt@caveimages.com
**Website** http://www.caveimages.com
**p.**16, 17, 22, 23, 65, 152

### Eric Dinyer
Eric Dinyer Imaging
8974 Cedar Drive
Shawnee Mission, KS 66207
**Phone** 913-642-6607
**Fax** 913-642-5006
**Email** dinyr@gvi.net
**Website** http://www.dreamless.com
**p.**130, 134, 135, 136, 137, 138, 141, 148

### Jeff Dungfelder
Studio DNA
117 E. Colorado Blvd./Suite 308
Pasadena, CA 91105
**Phone** 626-683-3078
**Fax** 626-683-3080
**Email** werk@studio-dna.com
**Website** http://www.studio-dna.com
**p.**60, 64, 125, 160

### Ronald Dunlap
Doglight Studios
600 Moulton Avenue/Suite 302
Los Angeles, CA 90031
**Phone** 213-222-1928
**Fax** 213-222-8151
**Email** doglight@aol.com
**Website** http://www.dogboys@doglight.com
**p.**98, 102, 103

# Artist's Directory Index

## Stephen Farrell
Slip Studios
4820 North Seeley Avenue/Floor 3
Chicago, IL 60625
**Phone** 773-989-0460
**Fax** 773-989-0460
**Email** SlipStudios@compuserve.com
**p.164, 166, 167**

## Scott Ferguson
Ferguson & Katzman Photography Inc.
710 N. Tucker / #512
St. Louis, MO 63101
**Phone** 314-241-3811
**Fax** 314-241-3087
**Email** fkphoto@ix.netcom.com
**p.38, 44, 45, 46, 137, 139**

## Rafael Peixoto Ferreira
Rafa Ferreira Design
Av. Orosimbo Maia 2090 a17
Campinas, SP 13024-030 Brazil
**Phone** 55-019-255-4985
**Fax** 55-019-255-4985
**Email** rfdesign@dglnet.com.br
**Website** http://radar.dglnet.com.br/
rafael/design
**p.78, 84, 85, 107**

## Dale Graham
ouch
P.O Box 603198
Providence, RI 02904
**Phone** 401-331-7141
**Fax** 401-331-5393
**Email** ouches@aol.com
**p.58, 62, 63, 87**

## Peter Gudynas
Zap Art
89 Hazelwell Cresent, Stirchley
Birmingham, B30 2QE England, UK
**Phone** 0121-459-0080
**Phone Rep.** 908-813-8718
**Fax** 908-813-0076
**Email** peter@zapart.demon.co.uk
**Website** http://dbl.ntticc.or.jp:
13000/InterServ/adb/new/OPENE.quest
**p.140, 144**

## Kip Henrie
Kip Henrie Illustration
610 E. 250 N.
Centerville, UT 84014
**Phone** 801-299-1567
**Fax** 801-299-1567
**Email** khenrie@aros.net
**p.36, 40, 65**

## John J. Hill
52mm Inc.
12 John Street / 10th Floor
New York, NY 10038
**Phone** 212-766-8035
**Fax** 212-766-8035
**Email** jinn@52mm.com
**Website** http://www.52mm.com
**p.50, 56, 57, 150**

## Lisa Johnston
digital wave imaging
2008 Rutger Street
St. Louis, MO 63104
**Phone** 314-436-0901
**Email** lisa@digitalwave.org
**Website** http://www.digitalwave.org/exhibit/
**p.20, 36, 42, 43, 161**

## Ramina Khachi
Khachi Design Group
1022 West Taylor
San Jose, CA 95126
**Phone** 408-298-9636
**Fax** 408-275-6529
**Email** ramina@rkdesign.com
**Website** http://www.rkdesign.com
**p.80, 82, 156, 157**

## Lax Syntax Design
Lance Jackson
19 Los Amigos Court
Orinda, CA 94563
**Phone** 510-253-3131
**Fax** 510-253-3191
**Email** lsd@ccnet.com
**Website** http://www.ccnet.com/~lsd
http://www.theispot.com/artist/ljackson
**p.70, 74, 75, 76, 77, 124, 159**

# Artist's Directory Index

**Michael Morgenstern**
429 East 73rd Street
New York, NY 10021
**Phone** 212-861-7391
**Email** threefish@aol.com
**Website** www.theispot.com/artist.morgenstern
p.120, 122, 123, 126, 127

**Seppo K. Niiranen**
Pix Productions
Kustaantie 27 A 4
Vantaa, 01400 Finland
**Phone** 358-0-050-5921217/Mobile
**Fax** 358-0-451-2096
**Email** skn@hut.fi
**Website** http:www.hut.fi/~skniiran
p.110, 112, 113, 114, 115, 125, 158

**Greg Pascos**
Dough-Boy Productions, Inc.
102 Bloor Street West
Toronto, M5S 1M8 Canada
**Phone** 416-968-0513
**Website** http://www.inforamp.net/~doughboy
p.18, 26, 27, 54, 150

**Scott W. Petty**
Bee Hive Design
11991 Driftstone Drive
Fishers, IA 46038
**Phone** 317-842-2412
**Fax** 317-842-2412
**Email** spetty@iei.net
p.15, 23, 132

**Lanny R. Quarles**
Solipsis International
2810 SE Franklin
Portland, OR 97202
**Phone** 503-234-5996
**Email** solipsis@hevanet.com
**Website** http://www.hevanet.com/solipsis
p.68, 72, 73, 74

**John Ritter**
John Ritter Illustration
228 Kingsbury Drive
Aptos, CA 95003
**Phone** 408-662-0273
**Fax** 408-662-0273
**Email** jritterill@aol.com
p.86, 87, 92, 140, 141, 142, 149

**Tony Schanuel**
Schanuel Photography
1706 St. Andrews Drive
O'Fellon, IL 62269
**Phone** 618-632-8550
**Phone** St. Louis 314-849-3495
**Fax** 618-624-1473
**Email** wtao@inlink.com
p.48, 52, 53, 160

**Ben Tomita**
Ben-An
2-9-8 Izumi, Suginami-Ku
Tokyo, 168-0063 Japan
**Phone** 03-3322-5887/003-5376-7618
**Fax** 03-3322-5833
**Email** @benan.com
**Website** http://www.benan.com
p.154, 163

**Anastasia Vasilakis**
153 East 96th Street/#4E
New York, NY 10128
**Phone** 212-348-4193
**Fax** 212-348-4193
**Email** studioav@earthlink.net
**Website** http://www.artarea.com
p.88, 94, 95, 96, 97, 135, 148

**Paul Watson**
Paul Watson Illustration
512 Lansdowne Avenue/Studio #7
Toronto, Ontario M6H 343 Canada
**Phone** 416-535-2648
**Fax** 416-535-2648
**Email** watson@passport.ca
p.26, 30, 54, 55, 66, 67

# New Digital Graphic Books
# From Dimensional Illustrators, Inc.

## ExtremeGraphics

Edited by: Kathleen Ziegler and Nick Greco

Digital creatives reach far beyond the limits of cyberspace in this premiere publication of **ExtremeGraphics**, a benchmark collection of electronic imagery. Experience the infinite capabilities of the computer as more than 300 full-color images break graphic rules and shatter your concept of reality. More than 30 digital visionaries featured in **ExtremeGraphics** exemplify the limitless possibilities of the new-media generation. Each provocative image transforms reality and illusion into a shifting, quixotic vision never before imagined. Journey beyond the limits of the known visual universe. **ExtremeGraphics** will propel you through the creative cosmos of cyberspace, exceed the limits of your expectations and push them to the extreme.

*Cover Image: Michael Morgenstern*

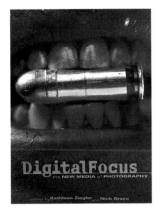

## DigitalFocus *The New Media of Photography*

Edited by: Kathleen Ziegler and Nick Greco

Experience the powerful imagery of digital photography. **DigitalFocus** explores the essence of both the explosive and impressive fusion of photography and digital illustration. This premiere edition applauds the diversity of this photographic genre and alters forever our perception of the camera and the computer. With more than 300 full-color examples, **DigitalFocus** discusses inventive software techniques, exposing the interrelationships that exist between the origin of the idea, the creative process, and the final image. This is a vital publication for all creative visionaries seeking to explore the cyber-technology of new media photography. Chapters include: Advertising, Business, Sports, Surreal, People, Editorial and Media.

*Cover Image: Nick Koudis*

## Digitalink *digital design and advertising*

Edited by: Kathleen Ziegler and Nick Greco

Take a quantum leap into the electrifying age of digital design and advertising. Immerse yourself in the cutting-edge genius of computer-generated imagery. Witness the fresh, raw enthusiasm of the digital illustrator. In this showcase edition of **Digitalink**, you will find more than 300 captivating digital illustrations in which the ingenuity of electronic art and advertising collide. Each provocative chapter explodes with details on the software, methods and techniques that shift electronic design into high gear. This book will both inspire and excite you as you delve into the limitless potential of this new-wave media. Chapters include: Magazine and Editorial Advertising, Direct Mail, Posters, Annual Reports, Book Covers and Brochures.

# New Step-By-Step Books
# From Dimensional Illustrators, Inc.

## CyberPalette
### A Digital Step-By-Step Guide
Edited by: Kathleen Ziegler and Nick Greco

**CyberPalette A Digital Step-By-Step Guide** features the artistry of 10 leading electronic design creatives. Each digital illustrator presents a methodical sequence of steps designed to divulge each facet of his or her creative process, layer by layer, from conceptual idea to final output image. Discover the techniques and software these artists use to achieve their astounding art. **CyberPalette** is an exceptional electronic pictorial presentation designed to stimulate your creative digital energies. Experience the infinite possibilities of the new-age technology and enter the fascinating realm of computer-generated artistry: Let your imagination soar through cyberspace.

*Cover Images: Ben Tomita, Pamela Hobbs (Inserts)*

## More Paper Sculpture
### A Step-By-Step Guide
Edited by: Kathleen Ziegler and Nick Greco

Expand your creative capabilities and experience a fascinating journey through the enchanting realm of paper sculpture. Ten internationally distinguished artists present all-new, hand selected projects and gallery pieces culled from their personal portfolios. This full-color, step-by-step guide features more than 300 photographs, from layout to finished sculpture. **More Paper Sculpture** is a valuable resource for the novice or professional seeking a delightful medium for artistic expression. Stimulate your creative energies and expand your marketability in the illustration and fine art industries. This absorbing and inspirational edition reveals the technical skills used by professional paper sculptors for enjoyment, as well as, for profit.

*Cover Image: Carol Jeanotilla*

| QUANTITY – TITLE | PRICE | – INT'L SHIPPING ADD $5.00 – PA RESIDENTS ADD 7% – | TOTAL |
|---|---|---|---|
| – Cyber Palette | $32.95 | | |
| – More Paper Sculpt. | $32.95 | | |

## Shipping Address: (Please Print Clearly)

Name_____

Firm_____

Address_____

City_____ State_____ Zip_____ (Country)_____

_____Check (drawn on a U.S. bank only)  _____Visa/MasterCard  _____MoneyOrder

Credit Card#_____

Signature_____ Exp.Date_____

Phone_____

### Send Payment to:
**Dimensional Illustrators, Inc.**
**362 2nd Street Pike/Suite 112**
**Southampton, PA 18966 USA**

215-953-1415 Phone
215-953-1697 Fax (24 hours)
dimension@3dimillus.com Email
3dimillus.com Online Orders
*U.S. Orders Shipped in 2 weeks.*
*Overseas orders shipped in 4-6 weeks.*

# ExtremeGraphics
## Call For Entries

Digital creatives reach far beyond the limits of cyber-space in this invitation only publication, a benchmark collection of electronic imagery. The digital visionaries featured in **ExtremeGraphics** exemplify the limitless possibilities of the new-media generation. Thirty new visionaries will be selected to showcase their work in next year's edition. Exceed the limits of your expectations and push them to the extreme.

### Preparation of Materials
Send Artwork for review on disk, slides, transparencies, photographic or laser prints. All work will be returned provided pre-paid packaging is provided.

### Deadline
Entries are accepted all year round.
Annual Deadline for submissions is **December 15**.

### Send To:
Nick Greco
**Dimensional Illustrators, Inc.**
362 2nd Street Pike / Suite 112
Southampton, PA 18966
215-953-1415 **Phone**
215-953-1697 **Fax**
dimension@3dimillus.com **Email**
http://www.3Dimillus.com **Website**

# Dimensional Illustrators, Inc.

**ExtremeGraphics** was produced by Dimensional Illustrators, Inc., a Philadelphia-based graphic arts publisher, to promote, honor and acknowledge excellence in the digital design industry. This premiere publication showcases the extreme edge of creative imagery in the electronic genre of the 21st century.

Principals Kathleen Ziegler and Nick Greco established Dimensional Illustrators, Inc., to support excellence in the advertising and publishing media. Since 1989, they have produced the 3Dimensional Illustrators Awards Show and have published several books featuring contemporary illustration, graphics, design and advertising, including **Digitalink, DigitalFocus, CyberPalette: A Digital Step-By-Step Guide** and **More Paper Sculpture: A Step-By-Step Guide**.

An accomplished illustrator and lecturer, Kathleen Ziegler is the creative director of **ExtremeGraphics**. Ms. Ziegler, the recipient of several graphics awards, has been featured in S**tep-By-Step Graphics** magazine, and has recently appeared on **Lifetime** and the **Home and Garden** TV networks.

Nick Greco is the executive editor of **ExtremeGraphics** and is responsible for marketing, researching and promoting future publications. Mr. Greco has lectured in the United States and the United Kingdom on copyright laws and the shared responsibilities of visual creatives and clients.